With The British Army In The Holy Land

H. O. Lock

Printing Statement:

Due to the very old age and scarcity of this book,
many of the pages may be hard to read due to the
blurring of the original text, possible missing pages,
missing text, dark backgrounds and other issues
beyond our control.

Because this is such an important and rare work, we
believe it is best to reproduce this book regardless of
its original condition.

Thank you for your understanding.

With the British Army in the Holy Land

BY

MAJOR H. O. LOCK

THE DORSETSHIRE REGIMENT

WITH MAPS

LONDON: ROBERT SCOTT

ROXBURGHE HOUSE

PATERNOSTER ROW, E.C.

1919

CONTENTS

v

CHAPTER XI

CHAPTER XII

CHAPTER XIII

CHAPTER XIV

CHAPTER XV

CHAPTER XVI

CHAPTER XVII

CHAPTER XVIII

SKETCH MAPS

NOTE

MY aim in compiling this little book has been to provide a short account of the Palestine campaign, illustrated from the experiences of one who was present.

The manuscript was written on active service, soon after the occurrence of the events recorded. It may, on this account, be sketchy, but, it is hoped, not the less interesting.

My acknowledgments are due to the Official Despatches and publications, and also to the writings of Mr. W. T. Massey, Official Correspondent with the Egyptian Expeditionary Force.

H. O. L.

In the Field, 1918.

WITH THE BRITISH ARMY IN THE HOLY LAND

CHAPTER I

EGYPT AND THE SUEZ CANAL

THE Holy Land has been the scene of war since the dawn of History. Long before Belgium became the cockpit of Europe, Palestine was the cock-pit of the known world. Here, on the high road between Asia and Africa, were fought the great wars of Egyptians and Assyrians, Israelites and Canaanites, Greeks and Romans, Saracens and Crusaders. With these few square miles are associated the names of the world's greatest soldiers no less than that of the Prince of Peace. None can fail to be interested in the latest campaign in this Land of Armageddon.

To understand the causes and events that led up to the campaign in Palestine of 1917-1918, we must first summarize, as shortly as possible, the modern history of Egypt. That country had for many centuries formed an integral part of the Turkish Empire. But she had been rapidly slipping from the grasp of the Turk. Early in the nineteenth century Mohamed Ali had effectually thrown off the Turkish yoke. True, the Turkish suzerainty remained; but that authority was little more than nominal and was represented by an annual money tribute paid to the Porte by the Khedive out of the revenues of Egypt.

Both France and England had large financial interests in Egypt, especially after the construction of the Suez Canal, which was opened for traffic in 1869.

The Suez Canal, in fact, became of vital importance to Great Britain. By a stroke of policy the British Government acquired the shares of the almost bankrupt Khedive, Ismail Pasha, and thus had a holding in the company worth several million pounds. But far more important to Britain was the position of the Canal as the great artery of the British Empire, the most vulnerable point on the short sea route to India. Thus Britain became directly concerned in the affairs of Egypt, in its internal administration to secure peace within, and in its military defence to secure the country in general, and the Canal zone in particular, from invasion by a foreign enemy.

But the affairs of Egypt were in a most unsatisfactory condition. The army was wholly unreliable, and extravagance in high places had brought the exchequer to the verge of bankruptcy. In 1882 matters reached a crisis. A revolution broke out, headed by Arabi Pasha, and the situation looked desperate. Joint naval and military action by Britain and France was proposed, but the French ships sailed away and left Britain with a free hand. The British fleet bombarded the Forts at Alexandria and a military force, based on the Suez Canal, was landed at Ismailia. This force completely defeated the army of Arabi Pasha at Tel-el-Kebir, put down the rebellion, and restored the government of the then Khedive, Tewfik Pasha. But the Khedivial government had been unable to cope with the rebellion single-handed ; it had only been restored to power by British arms ; it could not hope to retain that power unless continuously backed by the power of Britain.

From this time forward, whether she liked it or not, Britain found herself effectually saddled with the direction of the government of Egypt. In this position she became more fully confirmed by the Anglo-Egyptian military operations against the Soudan in 1885, under Gordon, and in 1898, under Kitchener. Outstanding differences with France were dispelled on the conclusion of the Anglo-French Entente Cordiale, and Britain was left virtually mistress of Egypt.

Let us look for a minute at the military geography of Egypt, particularly with regard to the security of her frontiers from invasion. Egypt consists, or prior to the seventies consisted, of the Nile, its valley and delta, and the country rendered fertile by that river. On either side of this fertile belt is dry, barren desert. On the north is the Mediterranean Sea, and on the south the tropical Soudan. Thus, in the hands of a power that holds the command of the sea, Egypt is well adapted for defence. The tropical Soudan makes a well-nigh impossible line of advance for a large hostile force from the south, and the routes of approach from the east and from the west, across the waterless deserts, present obstacles scarcely less formidable. Since the seventies, however, another important factor has entered the problem, namely, the Suez Canal and the area of cultivation and civilization which has sprung up along its banks. The large amount of fresh water required for the maintenance of the Canal, for the use of the towns that have sprung up along its banks, and for the existence of the large population which the Canal has attracted, is brought by a Canal known as the Sweet Water Canal, from the river Nile. This Sweet Water Canal, and the piped services which it supplied, were, in 1914, wholly upon the western or Egyptian side of the Suez Canal. This western side was also well provided with communications. Trunk railways connected Ismailia, at the centre of the Canal, with Cairo and Alexandria, and lateral railways, running along the whole length of the Canal, connected it with Port Said and Suez.

Although, as was subsequently discovered, the problem of defending the Suez Canal was by no means the same as that of defending Egypt, the problems may, at first sight, appear identical. An enemy force moving from Palestine against the Suez Canal and Egypt, would have to cross a comparatively waterless desert for a distance of over a hundred miles. On coming into collision with the defenders of the Canal, such an enemy would be operating far from his base, with a long and vulnerable line of communications, and with little or no available fresh water. The defenders, operating along the line of the Suez Canal, would be close to their base, with admirable communications, both lateral and to the rear, and with the rich cultivated lands of Egypt on which to draw for supplies, whilst their supply of fresh water would be unlimited.

The boundary line between Egypt and Palestine in 1914 ran from Rafa, on the Mediterranean, to the head of the Gulf of Akaba, the north-eastern arm of the Red Sea. This line runs right across the desert and is distant about 120 miles from the Suez Canal. At first sight the boundary seems ideal, and in so far as the defence of Egypt alone was concerned, it left little or nothing to be desired. But, as subsequent events proved, this line was not good enough to safeguard the defences of the Canal.

On the outbreak of war, in August, 1914, between Germany and Austria-Hungary on the one hand, and Great Britain, France, Russia and Belgium on the other, the garrison of Egypt was augmented by troops sent out from England and India and from Australia. The Suez Canal, through which vast numbers of troops were passing, was of vital importance to the communications of the allies, and was strongly guarded accordingly. Two months later (November 5), Turkey threw in her hand with the Central Powers. One of the baits held out by Germany to induce the Turks to enter the struggle, was a promise that they should be restored to complete supremacy in Egypt. With the entering of Turkey into the war, and her open threats to invade Egypt, the protection of that country and of the Canal became a matter of extreme urgency.

The policy of defence adopted was that of making the line of the Canal the line of resistance. A large portion of the low-lying desert to the north-east of the Canal was flooded, so as to render approach by that direction impossible. Warships took up stations in the Canal itself, while naval patrol launches took over the duty of guarding the Bitter Lakes. The troops detailed for the defence of the Canal itself were entrenched upon the western side, with reserves concentrated at points of tactical importance. In this way full advantage was taken of the lateral communications on the western side of the Canal, while it was thought that the difficulties of crossing the desert on the eastern side would make approach by the Turks well-nigh impossible.

Meanwhile, the Turk was not letting the grass grow under his feet. Whether the Germans ever intended to pay the price for Turkish adhesion by sending a strong enough force to make the invasion of Egypt practicable is open to doubt. The Turkish rank and file were certainly led to believe that a serious invasion of Egypt was intended. But it is much more likely that the object of the Germans was to detain as large a British force as possible in Egypt and thus prevent their taking part in the fighting in France. A secondary object may have been to render the Suez Canal temporarily impassable. Whatever may have been the chestnuts that Germany hoped to get out of the fire, it was clear that Turkey was willing to act as catspaw, and attempt a foolhardy invasion of Egypt. Consequently, the construction of a new military railway in Syria was put in hand, and by January, 1915, the Turks had formed advanced posts at Auja, on the frontier, and also at Kosseima, El Arish, and Khan Epenus in the desert. The problem of water supply has always presented a difficulty to armies crossing this waterless desert. There are a certain number of reservoirs and cisterns which hold up water during the rains. In the winter time these would be full. The Turk is less particular about the water which he drinks than the white man, and doubtless he could, to some extent, be supplied from some of the brackish pools in the

desert, with water that no one would think of offering to
British soldier.

The light pontoons that the Turks dragged across the dese
for crossing the Canal are said to have been used for carryir
water during certain stages of the advance. Suffice it to sa
that the Turks did succeed in solving the water problem, ar
in crossing the desert with a force of some considerable strengtl

On the 3rd February, 1915, the threatened attack materialize
Before dawn, some of the light pontoons which the Turks ha
brought with them, were launched on the Canal. These we
manned, while other Turks deployed along the eastern ban
and opened fire to cover the crossing. The troops defendin
this portion of the Canal, mostly Indians, opened fire upon ti
pontoons, with the result that many of them were sunk. Tw
of the pontoons, however, reached the western bank, and the
crews, numbering about twenty, surrendered. There wa
fighting throughout the day, but no further crossing of th
Canal. On the next day the east bank was swept, with th
result that a considerable party of the enemy were capturec
After this, the Turks withdrew, and marched back to Palestin
This was the only time that a formed body of the enem
succeeded in reaching the Canal. But they had shown tha
it was possible for them to achieve the almost impossibl
and thus they gave the authorities responsible for the defenc
of Egypt much food for thought.

The menace to Egypt was for a time delayed, though nc
wholly removed, by the expedition against the Dardanelles.

To co-operate with our Russian allies, the British Goverr
ment decided, early in 1915, to attempt to force the passag
of the Dardanelles. The strategic gains promised were highl
attractive, and included--the passage of arms and munitior
from the allies to Russia in exchange for wheat, the neutralit
and possible adherence of the outstanding Balkan States, th
severing of communications between European and Asiat
Turkey, the drawing off of Turkish troops from the theatres c

he war, and the expulsion of the Turks from Constantinople,
and ultimately from Europe. Incidentally, it was considered,
on the principle that the best defensive is an offensive, that a
thrust at the very heart of Turkey, a threat against Constantinople itself, would afford the best means of defending Egypt.

The story of the Dardanelles expedition has been often told,
and scarcely forms a part of this history, so a few words must
suffice. In February, 1915, we started by bombarding the
forts with a few old warships. The forts at the outer entrance
were soon silenced, and early in March, the warships moved
up to the Narrows. On the 18th, a great effort was made to
reduce the forts about the Narrows; but it failed, with the
loss of three battleships and more than 2,000 men. This
demonstrated the fact that the Dardanelles could never be
opened by sea power alone, and, accordingly, amphibious
operations became necessary. An expeditionary force was
assembled in Egypt, and Mudros was selected as the advanced
base. On April 25, landings were effected on the extreme
point of the Gallipoli Peninsula. In spite of heroic attempts,
we did little more than effect a precarious lodgment. Further
operations were necessary; additional divisions were brought
out from home; and on the night of the 6th/7th August,
another landing was effected at Suvla Bay. But the new plan
was no more successful than the old. Within a couple of
days this force also had settled down to a war of positions.
Winter was approaching; our positions on the peninsula
would then become no longer tenable. No progress could be
made, and at length it was decided to evacuate. The Suvla
Bay force was withdrawn first; and the evacuation of the
main body of troops was completed on the 20th December.
The withdrawal was carried out with the same brilliance that
had characterized the various landings, and with so small a
number of casualties that it was described as " an achievement
without parallel in the annals of war."

Many of the regiments that fought against the Turks at

Gallipoli were withdrawn, directly or indirectly to Egypt, an
subsequently met the Turk again during the advance in
Palestine. Included among these were the 10th, 52nd, 53r
and 54th Divisions, besides regiments of Anzacs and Yeomanr
In so far as the Dardanelles operations aimed at protectin
Egypt, they were a success ; for, while they were in progres
no organized invasion of Egypt was attempted. But th
evacuation had the effect of liberating a large force of Turkey
best troops for operations against Mesopotamia and Egypt.

It would be convenient to pause here and take stock of th
military situation in Egypt, in the light of over a year's exper
ence of actual war.

In the first place, the Turks had disillusioned us as to th
impossibility of crossing the waterless desert, and had actuall
crossed it with a considerable armed and organized forc
They announced that what they had effected had been nothin
more than a reconnaissance. In any case, they had show
us what they could do, and that, backed by the resources
the Central Powers, there would be no insuperable obstac
to their bringing a large and fully equipped army across t
desert.

In the second place, we had discovered that the problen
of defending the Suez Canal and of defending Egypt were n
identical. While the Canal formed an admirable moat, a
obstacle difficult to negotiate when stoutly defended, and so
capital defensive line for the protection of the Nile ; yet th
line was inadequate for the protection of the Canal itself
for securing the immunity of the passing shipping.

And so, thirdly, we realized that some other line must
found for the protection of the Canal. While we were sitti
on the west bank, small parties of Turks approached t
eastern bank. On more than one occasion, in the summ
of 1915, they succeeded in placing mines in the fairway of t
Canal. It would, therefore, have been quite possible for the
to have seriously interfered with the working of the Can

and the passage of shipping. Granted that a new line must be found, the question arises where such new line should be drawn. A line across the actual desert may be all very well in war time, though none too easy to hold, for the reasons that we have already discussed. But to keep a garrison on such a line for ever would be well-nigh intolerable. Thus, by a process of elimination, we find that the most suitable line for the permanent defence of the Suez Canal is the fertile country beyond the eastern desert—in other words, Palestine.

Fourthly, it had been brought home to us that the worst form of defence is a passive defence. As, therefore, the Turk would not leave well alone, but insisted on attacking us in Egypt, so it became necessary for us to meet him on his own ground, to push a vigorous offensive, and eventually to carry the war into Palestine.

CHAPTER II

THE DESERT OF SINAI

IN accordance with the policy of defending the Suez Canal upon a line further east, the construction of a new defensive line was put in hand during the early months of 1916. No longer were the Turks to be allowed to annoy us by actually reaching the Canal. A line of trenches, protected by barbed wire entanglements, was constructed out in the desert, a few miles to the east of the Canal. As may be imagined, this was no easy task. A large amount of excavation was necessary for a small amount of trench ; walls had to be built up with sandbags ; and other steps had to be taken to prevent the sides from foundering, and to construct a work that would withstand shell fire.

Meanwhile, other preparations were put in hand for carrying the defensive line further to the east. The construction was commenced of a broad gauge of railway from Kantara eastwards across the desert. This railway eventually became the trunk line between Egypt and Palestine. In the days of trench warfare before Gaza, it transported freight trains heavily laden with rations and ammunitions, troop trains conveying officers and men in open trucks, hospital trains evacuating sick and wounded, and an all-sleeping-car express running nightly in each direction. In 1918, a swing-bridge was improvised across the Suez Canal, and Jerusalem and Cairo were then connected by rail without change of carriage being necessary. The future prospects of this railway seem unbounded. It will undoubtedly be continued through to Damascus and Aleppo, where it will connect with railways to Constantinople and to Baghdad and the Persian Gulf. Thus it will form part of a grand trunk railway system along the old caravan routes connecting the three continents of Europe, Asia, and Africa. In its conception, it was just a military railway, laid, with but little preparation, across the sands of the desert. To this railway, however, was largely due the success of the campaign that we are about to consider.

We have already seen that the Sinaitic Desert is almost waterless. Although it has often been crossed by invading armies in both directions, the provision of water has always presented the greatest difficulty. The carriage of water in tanks upon the backs of camels, a method used by us for locally supplying troops between water dumps and the headquarters of units, proved successful here thousands of years ago. The plan adopted by the Turks of dragging water-holding pontoons across the desert was not to be despised. Further progress was made when supplies of water were transported in tank-trucks along the railway. But a bolder adaptation of modern science to desert fighting was reached, when it was decided to lay on a piped supply of water from the Nile.

We have seen that the western bank of the Suez Canal was already provided with a plentiful supply of fresh water by the Sweet Water Canal. Plant was now installed for making this water available for the troops. Purity had to be considered as well as adequacy of supply. A peculiar danger had to be guarded against. There is a disease prevalent in Egypt, of a particularly unpleasant character and persistent type, called by the medical profession Bilhaziosis, but better known to our men as " Bill Harris." This disease is conveyed by a parasitic worm found in the waters of the Nile, and affects not only those who drink the water, but also those who bathe in it or merely wash. Consequently, orders were stringent against even touching Nile water which had not previously been treated. This necessitated the troops east of the Canal being put upon a very restricted supply, and they were accordingly rationed at the rate of a gallon of water per head per day for all purposes, including washing, cooking and drinking. At the Kantara waterworks water was drawn in from the Sweet Water Canal, mixed with alum, and pumped through settling tanks into filters. When it had passed through these, it was pumped underneath the Suez Canal into reservoirs on the eastern bank. Here it was chlorinated; and hence the water, now fit for all purposes, was pumped forward to its destination. There being no gradient to assist the natural flow of the water, it had to be pumped forward by successive stages. The first stage was as far as Romani; when working at greatest length the pumping stages numbered no less than seventeen. At times, during the advance, the railway had to be called in aid; and train-loads of water for the use of advanced troops were railed from pipe-head up to rail-head. At some stages of the advance this supply could be supplemented by local water, which, though generally somewhat brackish, was employed for the horses, mules and camels. It was even found to have no ill-effect upon the troops, if used for a limited period, and if necessary precautions were taken. At other stages, where water was non-existent, or rendered wholly unapproachable by enemy dispositions, our force became entirely dependent upon the supply delivered through the pipe-line. Ultimately, when we settled down to protracted trench warfare before Gaza, this pipe-line was delivering a constant supply of water into our trenches, distant some couple of hundred miles from the banks of the Nile.

Kantara started upon a process of development worthy of the base of such an expedition. Before the war, it had been little more than a small Canal village, comprising a few huts. It eventually grew into an important railway terminus with wharves and cranes, a railway ferry and 40 miles of sidings. Miles of first-class macadamized roads were made, vast ordnance and supply dumps arose, and camps and depots were

stablished for man and beast. The scale on which this
mushroom town developed was stupendous.

Early in 1916, the Turks, relieved from imminent danger
near home by our evacuation of Gallipoli, came down again
in force through Syria, Palestine and the Desert, to attack
us in Egypt. Our construction gangs, engaged upon the new
railway and upon the development of local water supplies,
were at this time covered by escorts, mainly of cavalry, spread
out upon a wide front. On the 23rd of April several thousand
Turks, operating in three columns, attacked our desert posts
at Oghratina, Katia and Dueidar respectively, the two former
being about 30 miles and the last named about 10 miles to
the east of Kantara. Oghratina and Katia, being well out in
the desert, were cavalry posts held by yeomanry. These two
posts were rushed by a large force of the enemy under cover
of fog, and, though a stubborn resistance was offered, and the
fighting was severe, the posts were overwhelmed. At Dueidar,
an infantry post, some 20 miles or so nearer our base, the
Turk was less successful. Under cover of the same fog, about
100 Turks tried to rush this post at dawn. They found the
garrison standing to, and were beaten off. Though they made
three distinct attempts to break through, they were unsuccess-
ful. The garrison was reinforced and the Turks were repulsed.

In order to hamper or prevent such bodies of Turks from
again crossing the desert and approaching the Canal, it was
decided to draw off the local water supplies in the desert.
Accordingly, these supplies, mainly in pools and cisterns constructed by men in a bygone age, were systematically pumped
or drained dry. By the end of June, no water was left available for enemy use within easy reach of the Canal. From this
time forward the enemy attempted no more sporadic raids.
He concentrated instead upon a serious attack against our
main positions, which attack materialized at Romani.

By July, 1916, our railway had reached the village of Romani,
which is some 25 miles from Kantara, and is in the neighbour-

hood of Oghratina and Katia, where the enemy had secure
his success in April. The Turkish force had been stiffened
with Germans and Austrians, and was under the command
of the German General Von Kressenstein. It moved from th
Turkish railroad at Auja on the frontier, and advanced by way
of Maghdaba and the Wadi El Arish to El Arish, and thenc
westward along the caravan route towards Egypt. Thi
force had been well equipped and trained for this class o
warfare, and it succeeded in dragging heavy guns across th
desert by roads which it improvised for the purpose. Making
his advanced base at Bir-el-Abd, the enemy first occupied an
fortified a line about Mageiba. On the morning of the 3rd
August, he made a general advance, and took up a line front
ing our position at Romani. Here our left flank rested on th
sea ; the left of the line was held by the 52nd Division, whil
the 53rd Division was on the right. The East Lancashir
Division was in reserve. The right flank comprised a chai
of posts, behind which were a force of cavalry. The weal
point was, therefore, our right flank, for a little force workin,
round by the south would threaten our communications an
might possibly cut us off from our reinforcements down th
line and from our base at Kantara. Accordingly, on the nigh
of the 3rd/4th, one Light Horse Brigade moved out to hold
three miles line from our infantry post on the right, sendin
out patrols a considerable distance in front. About midnigh
the enemy were found to be advancing in this direction. Be
fore light next morning this Brigade were heavily engaged
holding up the advance of a considerable body of the enemy
Gradually the Brigade were pressed back by weight of number:
until, at about five o'clock in the morning, the timely arriva
of reinforcements secured the complete arrest of the enem
advance in this direction. Soon after daylight the enem
swung round his left flank and established himself upon Moun
Royston. This enforced upon us a further retirement ; bu
he had reached the limit of his success. Towards the sea, th

enemy attacks against the 52nd Division were beaten off, and here he could make no progress. At about 5.30 in the afternoon, a counter-attack was launched against Mount Royston, and this position was recaptured. Early on the following morning, the 5th, before daylight, the 52nd Division recaptured Wellington Ridge, the last of our lost positions remaining in the hands of the Turk. The tide had now turned definitely in our favour and the Turk was in full retreat. An attempt was made to encircle his southern flank and to cut him off with our cavalry, but his rearguard actions were fought stubbornly, and the pursuing cavalry had to be withdrawn. During the night of the 5th/6th, the enemy evacuated Katia, which was occupied by us on the following morning. By the 8th, he had abandoned Oghratina, and had fallen back to his advanced base at Bir-el-Abd. From this base he now proceeded to evacuate camps and stores, but he was not allowed to do so unmolested. He was followed up by the whole of our cavalry and effectually shelled by our horse artillery. On the afternoon and evening of this day (the 8th) the Turk counter attacked our cavalry, who were clearly outnumbered. Nevertheless the Turk considered it more prudent to burn the remainder of his stores. He completed the evacuation of Abd by the 12th, and it remained in our hands from this time forward. This abortive advance against Romani marked the last determined attempt of the Turks to invade the Suez Canal and Egypt. Henceforth the efforts of the Turks were confined to opposing the storm which their misguided cupidity had raised up against them.

After the battle of Romani, our mounted troops held a line about Abd. The enemy now consolidated a position at Mazar, a little more than 20 miles further to the east. In the middle of September, a cavalry column moved out to Mazar and attacked the Turkish positions. Neither side was anxious to bring on a general engagement at that time. However, the losses which the Turk suffered in this operation caused him sufficient uneasiness to induce him to withdraw altogether from Mazar. He therefore withdrew his troops to a position close to El Arish.

The Turkish garrison at El Arish consisted of some 1,600 infantry in all, in a strong entrenched position. In the second week of December increased activity was shown by the Turks, and aerial reconnaissance of their camps behind their front line showed evidence of the proximity of reinforcements. Our preparations for a forward move were pressed on strenuously, and, though they were somewhat delayed through lack of water, we were ready to move by the 20th December. The enemy realized that the swiftness of our final preparations had been too much for him. Knowing that his reinforcements could not arrive in time, he hurriedly withdrew his troops from El Arish. This retirement was reported by the R.F.C. on the 20th December, and our mounted troops, supported by infantry, were ordered to move on El Arish the same night. The town was found to be evacuated. Aircraft reports showed that about 1,600 of the enemy were on the march, in two columns, in the neighbourhood of Maghdaba and Abu Aweigila, while Sheikh Zowaid and Rafa appeared to be clear. The enemy were evidently not retreating by the caravan route towards Gaza, but were falling back southwards by the Wadi El Arish (the Biblical " River of Egypt ") upon their railhead at Auja.

This evidence went to show that the garrison which had recently evacuated El Arish were at Maghdaba, and it seemed likely that this force were preparing to hold Maghdaba as a rearguard. A flying column of cavalry was immediately despatched against them from El Arish. This column found the enemy strongly posted and entrenched on both banks of the Wadi El Arish. An attack was set in motion on the morning of the 23rd December, and lasted for the greater part of the day. By half-past four that afternoon, however, all organized resistance was over, and the enemy were surrendering everywhere. No further advance was attempted along the enemy's line of communications towards Auja, and the troops, being but a flying column, retired at once to El Arish.

Within a few days after the destruction at Maghdaba of the rearguard, or garrison withdrawing from El Arish, another body of the enemy started to entrench a position at Magruntein near Rafa. This was obviously intended to bar our progress eastwards along the coastal route, the old caravan route to Gaza. Rafa is the frontier town upon the Turco-Egyptian frontier. The operation to which we are about to refer was, therefore, the last engagement that took place upon Egyptian territory. It was not possible at the end of December for the British force to push on and occupy Rafa permanently, owing to difficulties of supply. But since the enemy had again placed a small detached garrison within striking distance of our mounted troops, the temptation was held out for a repetition of the Maghdaba success at Magruntein. Accordingly, a flying column, composed wholly of mounted troops and artillery, moved out from El Arish on the evening of the 8th/9th January, 1917. The enemy was taken completely by surprise, and by dawn on the 9th January his position was almost entirely surrounded. The position, however, was a formidable one, with ground in front entirely open and devoid of cover. The main attack was timed for ten o'clock a.m., and was delivered from the east and south-east. The town of Rafa was soon occupied, and, in the course of the morning, our attack against the Turkish system of defences developed on every side. The enemy's works were dominated by a central redoubt or keep, and orders were given for a concerted attack to be developed against this at 3.30 p.m. Meanwhile the enemy had despatched a relieving force from Shellal, which is about twenty miles to the south-east of Rafa and mid-way between that town and the nearest Turkish railway. This relieving force was detected by our aircraft, who frequently attacked it with bombs and machine gun fire. Orders were at once given for the attack on the redoubt to be pressed with vigour, and, before five o'clock, the redoubt was captured. With this position in our hands, the remaining works soon fell, and by 5.30 p.m. all organized resistance was over, and the enemy position, with all its garrison, was captured. The relieving force were driven off without much difficulty, and withdrew, presumably, to Shellal, which thereafter became the enemy's next point of concentration. Our column, taking with them all prisoners, animals and captured material, withdrew again to El Arish.

From the time of our occupation of El Arish on the 22nd December, that town developed apace. Mine-sweeping operations were at once commenced in the roadstead, a pier was erected, and, on the 24th, the supply ships from Port Said began unloading stores and supplies. The lie of the land gives unlimited opportunity to a power having the command of the sea to supplement his other means of bringing forward supplies by landing sea-borne goods upon the open beach. Repeatedly, in the subsequent history of this war, we availed ourselves of this means of supply, as our army moved northwards in Palestine. The landing of stores at El Arish, however, was not wholly successful, owing to the strong currents, a shelving and shifting beach, and heavy surf. In winter, the sea is apt to be stormy here, and then such landing may become impossible. Supplies were also hastened to El Arish by camel convoy, and dumps were accumulated. The railway was pushed on with and, before the end of January, the railway station at El Arish was completed; during the following month the railway was pushed further out along the coast preparatory to another advance.

After the destruction of their post at Rafa, the Turks immediately began to concentrate their forces near Shellal. West of this place they prepared a strong defensive position near Weli Sheikh Nuran, with the object of covering their lines of communication both along the Beersheba railway and along

he Jerusalem-Hebron-Beersheba road. They also estab-
ished themselves at Khan Yunus, on the coastal road a few
niles to the east of Rafa. On the 23rd February, a reconnaissance was carried out against Khan Yunus. The column,
arriving at dawn, found the position strongly held, and,
after manoeuvring the enemy out of his front line of defence
and capturing prisoners, withdrew without difficulty. Continuous pressure maintained by our troops in this neighbourhood, however, induced the enemy to withdraw the garrison
of Khan Yunus, which place was entered by our cavalry without opposition on the 28th February. The enemy also evacuated without firing a shot the position which he had prepared
near Weli Sheikh Nura.

Our troops had crossed the desert with success attending
them at every stage. And now at last they had set foot in
the Promised Land. Many of them must have felt, what a
soldier was afterwards heard to express, "This may be the land
of promise ; it's certainly not the land of fulfilment." History
repeats itself. As the Israelites had much trial and suffering
to endure after reaching this stage of their journey from Egypt,
before they were permitted to " go in and possess the land,"
so had our lads many a fierce and bloody battle to fight before
they, too, might set foot within the Holy City.

A few words as to personnel may not be out of place before
we leave the subject of this Desert campaign. Throughout
this time the Commander-in-Chief of the Egyptian Expeditionary Force was General Sir Archibald Murray, G.C.M.G.,
K.C.B. A reorganization of the force took place in October,
1917, in consequence of which General Murray moved his
headquarters back from Ismailia to Cairo. At the same time,
the new headquarters of the Eastern Force came into existence at Ismailia under the command of Lieut.-General Sir
Charles Dobell, K.C.B., C.M.G., D.S.O., under whose direction thus came more immediately the operations in the eastern
desert.

Amongst the troops employed were the Australians and New Zealanders and several regiments of English Yeomanry, and included among the infantry, were the 52nd (Lowland), the 53rd (Welsh and Home Counties), the 54th (East Anglian) and the 74th (Dismounted Yeomanry) Divisions.

This review of the advance across the desert has of necessity been superficial. Strictly speaking, the Desert campaign is outside the scope of this book. But a summarized history of the advance forms a necessary introduction to our subject. Here, on the threshold of Palestine, we must leave this army for a short space, while we review some other operations, and while we take a glance at the nature of the country in which this army was about to operate.

CHAPTER III

MESOPOTAMIA, THE CAUCASUS, AND THE HEJAZ

HAVING taken a hurried glance at the campaign in Sinai, which directly led up to that in Palestine, we will take a yet more hurried glance at three other campaigns in Asiatic Turkey which had their bearing, direct or indirect, upon the Palestine operations.

Most important among these was the expedition to Mesopotamia. In 1914, when Turkey came into the war against us, a British Indian Brigade was landed at the mouth of the Shatt-el-Arab, the common estuary by which the Tigris and the Euphrates reach the Persian Gulf. The objects of this expedition were to secure the oil-fields of Persia in which Britain was largely interested ; to neutralize German ascendancy, which was rapidly developing in this part of the world through her interests in the Baghdad Railway ; and to embarrass Turkey by attacking her at a point where facilities of manœuvre and supply seemed to hold out a reasonable promise of success.

Throughout 1915 this expedition met with uninterrupted success. The British Indian forces engaged were increased in number and strength, and, in spite of appalling conditions of climate, and notwithstanding more than one narrow escape from disaster, the British flag was pushed further and further forward into this flat alluvial country. In the autumn of 1915, we held all the country up to Nasiriyeh on the Euphrates and to Kut el Amara on the Tigris. Then that ill-fated de-

cision was arrived at which sent General Townshend, with
the inadequate force at his command, up the Tigris to capture
Baghdad. This force went heroically forward, and, just short
of that city, defeated the Turks at the battle of Ctesiphon.
But General Townshend's casualties were heavy, and his
available reinforcements were neither sufficiently numerous
nor at hand. The pick of the Turkish army released by our
withdrawal from Gallipoli, had poured down to reinforce the
enemy, and General Townshend had no alternative but to
beat a hasty retreat. Accordingly, he fell back to Kut el
Amara. Partly from inability to get his war-worn forces
further away, and partly from a disinclination to abandon this
important tactical point to the enemy, he consolidated here
and prepared to withstand a siege. The history of that siege
will live as one of the noblest in the annals of the British army.
But the stars in their courses fought against us. Strong enemy
positions, inadequate supplies and transport arrangements,
floods, and appalling conditions of country and weather, proved
overwhelming. In spite of the unremitting efforts of the
relieving army, which fought battle after battle without stint
of labour or loss, the garrison of Kut found themselves, at the
beginning of May, 1916, left with no alternative but to capitu
late. Almost the whole of the garrison were removed into
Asia Minor, to a captivity which few were destined to survive.
Naturally the Turks were much elated by this success, following upon their successes in Gallipoli, and were persuaded that
the might of the British arm was nothing which they need fear.

Leaving a sufficient force to check any further British advance into Mesopotamia, the Turk withdrew the bulk of his
forces to operate against the Russians and, perhaps wisely,
made no great effort to dislodge us from the territory which
we already occupied. The opposing forces sat down and
watched each other for many months in the entrenched positions below Kut. In March of the following year, 1917,
General Maude, on whom had fallen the command of the

British army in Mesopotamia, won a decisive victory at Kut ; and, pursuing the remnants of the routed enemy, entered Baghdad. The Turks withdrew to the higher country north and north-east of the city, whither they were pursued. After these operations, the British were in occupation of the completed section of the Baghdad railway, which was then open from Baghdad as far north as Samarra. They also effected a junction with the Russian troops operating in Persia. In the following September, engagements were fought at Ramadi and elsewhere on the Euphrates, with the result that the Turkish garrisons were rounded up, and but few Turkish troops were left to oppose the British forces in Mesopotamia. Nevertheless, an immediate advance was not made up to Mosul and the upper territories of Mesopotamia. Owing to the collapse of Russia, it became necessary for us to take over some of the country in Persia, which had previously been occupied by Russian troops, and an expedition was also sent to assist the Armenians at Baku on the Caspian Sea. Other troops which could be spared from Mesopotamia were sent round, in the spring of 1918, to take part in the operations in Palestine, and the forces that remained were devoted to the garrisoning and consolidation of the territory already occupied.

A glance at the map of Turkey in Asia will show that the provinces of Mesopotamia and Syria consist of long narrow strips of fertile country bordered by desert, and resemble two legs which fork at Aleppo.

As far as Aleppo, troops and supplies from Europe passed over one common route. From the Turkish point of view, therefore, the campaigns in these two countries were to some extent interdependent. This enabled the Turks to concentrate a reserve at Aleppo, ready to be moved down into either theatre of war as the exigencies of the situation might demand. Conversely, therefore, a British offensive in Mesopotamia might draw off troops destined for Palestine, or an offensive in Palestine might attract troops otherwise intended for opera-

c

tions in Mesopotamia. There is strong evidence that a Turco
German offensive was contemplated in Mesopotamia for 1918
In the spring of that year, however, a British offensive wa
undertaken in Palestine, which had the immediate effect c
drawing to that country strong Turkish and German rein
forcements from Aleppo. Nothing more was heard of th
offensive in Mesopotamia, and, by the autumn of 1918, ther
was scarcely a fighting Turk to be found in that country
Just as our expedition against the Dardanelles, by engagin
the enemy at a vital spot near home, had materially assiste
the defence of Egypt, so did our offensives in Palestine mater
ally assist the defence of Mesopotamia.

Turning to another corner of the map of Turkey, wher
Europe and Asia meet in the mountains of the Caucasus, w
see that the Turkish frontier here marches with that of Russia
In the earlier days of the war, the Russians carried out a
important and successful advance in this neighbourhood, and
early in 1916, occupied the cities of Trebizond and Erzerum
Thus, at the time when the campaign in Palestine was embarke
upon, the armies of the allies were closing in upon Easter
Turkey simultaneously from three directions, the Russia
Caucasus army from the north-east, the British Mesopotamia
army from the south-east, and the Egyptian Expeditionar
Force from the south. Strategically, the situation seeme
full of promise. But, in the winter of 1917-18, followed th
disastrous collapse of Russia, and the setting free of man
Turkish soldiers of good quality from all the Russian front
for service elsewhere. We had hoped that our offensive i
Syria might have been supported by the co-operation of th
Russians. Instead, we felt the pinch of their defection i
the stiffening of enemy resistance on our front by the transfe
of good troops from the Caucasus to Palestine.

There is yet another theatre of warfare in Asiatic Turkey
the operations in which exerted considerable influence o
those in Palestine. The whole of the eastern shores of th

Red Sea formed part of the Ottoman Empire. The southernmost sector, known as the Yemen, was the farthest outpost of that Empire. Here a few Turks and Arabs conducted a sporadic warfare against our garrison at Aden, more calculated to cause annoyance and to detain a British force of some strength than to exercise much influence upon the war as a whole.

Farther to the north, on this Red Sea littoral, is a province of much more importance, the Hejaz, in which are situate the most holy of cities in the Moslem world, Mecca and Medina. To Christians, the Hejaz is forbidden ground. To Mahomedans, it is the focus of pilgrimage from all parts of the world. The Sultan of Turkey, as the ruler of Mecca, is looked up to by the Sunni or orthodox Mahomedans in all lands as the spiritual head of their Church. Though rulers of the Hejaz, the Turks were not at one with the local population. These are Arabs, and to them the Turkish rule was as unpopular as to most other non-Turkish subjects of that decaying Empire. Profiting by Turkey's embarrassments in other parts, the Arabs rose in the summer of 1916, resolved on ridding themselves of the hated Turkish yoke. Sheikh Hussein of Mecca was proclaimed King of the Hejaz.

At this time there were garrisons of Turkish troops stationed at Mecca, Medina and at the port of Jiddah. Their communication with Turkey was by the recently opened railway to Damascus and Aleppo. This railway, south of Damascus, ran along the high plateau on the eastern side of the Dead Sea, through Maan, and along the desert to Medina. The intention was to carry the line ultimately through to Mecca, but at this time it was only open for traffic as far as Medina. The revolt broke out on the 5th June, 1916, at which date a cordon was spread round Medina. Jiddah was attacked on the 9th, and capitulated after holding out for only a week. The bulk of the Mecca garrison were at this time at Taif. Accordingly, the town of Mecca passed into the hands of the

Emir, with the exception of the ports. These put up a sm
fight, but had all surrendered by the middle of July. T
force at Taif were blockaded, and, on the 23rd September, tl
force also surrendered. By this time, all the outlying garriso
had been disposed of, and the Hejaz generally cleared of Turl

Meanwhile, Medina had not only held out, but had be
reinforced, and the fighting strength brought up to son
14,000. Late in September, the Turks sallied out and esta
lished a cordon of posts at a distance of some 30 to 40 mil
from the city. They also pushed further afield ; but, Ar
armies moving up from the south, the Turks withdrew, at t
end of the year, behind the cordon of posts which they b
established. For the next six months, the railway to tl
north of Medina was frequently raided by the Arabs, but tl
town was effectually cut off from its communications wir
Turkey.

In July, 1917, Akaba, at the head of the gulf of that nam
the north-eastern arm of the Red Sea, was captured. Th
is at no great distance from Maan, an important depot on tl
Hejaz Railway, the last outpost of Syria at the edge of tl
desert of North Arabia. From Akaba, the railway was no
attacked at Maan, with serious results to Medina ; neverth
less, that city continued to hold out, and was probably nev
very closely invested.

In October and November, 1917, about the time of the thi
battle of Gaza, the Turks were still in Maan, and tried
assume the offensive against the Arabs, but proved too wea
to succeed. After the fall of Jerusalem, the Turks withdre
to some extent, and the Arabs advanced towards the lanc
east of the Dead Sea.

From this period forward, the history of the Hejaz revo
merges in that of the Palestine campaign. The Arab forc
east of the Dead Sea afforded a safeguard against any possib
Turkish attempt to move round our right flank and raid or
line of communications. In February and in March, 191

Turkish expeditions moving against the Arab forces of the King of the Hejaz southward from Kerak, near the south-eastern corner of the Dead Sea, met with failure. The former expedition ended in disaster, and the latter was forced to withdraw, owing to the imminence of a British crossing of the Jordan in its rear. Arab activity on the railway now definitely isolated Medina. Although the Arabs were never strong enough to push a powerful force up through Eastern Palestine, yet the presence of a friendly force operating in that country exercised considerable influence upon the later stages of the Palestine campaign. The assistance which the Arabs gave in the ultimate destruction of the Turkish army was invaluable.

CHAPTER IV

PALESTINE

THE story of a campaign is more interesting if we have a general idea of the topography of the country in which it is conducted. Our time will, therefore, not be wasted if we leave the British Army on the frontiers of the Holy Land for a few minutes longer and form a mental picture of the terrain over which they are about to operate.

Picture a country, about the size of Wales, divided into parallel strips running north and south, zones of alternate elevation and depression. This will give a rough idea of the conformation of Southern Palestine. On the west is the Mediterranean Sea. Skirting the sea are a series of sand dunes, beyond which comes the Coastal Plain. Together these form the first depressed strip, averaging about 15 miles in width. Northwards, it tapers to a point where the mountains reach the sea at Cape Carmel. Beyond the Coastal Plain is the range of mountains on which stands Jerusalem, the mountains of Samaria and of Judæa, rising to a height of about 3,000 feet above the level of the sea. On the eastern side of these mountains is a steep drop to the Valley of the Jordan and the Dead Sea, the level of the latter being nearly 1,300 feet below the level of the Mediterranean, and more than 4,000 feet below the summit of the adjoining Mount of Olives. Beyond the Jordan valley the country rises again abruptly into the hills of Moab or Eastern Palestine. Beyond lies the waterless desert.

Before entering into details, let us imagine ourselves to be

tanding on one of the mountains round about Jerusalem.[1]
way to the north, Mount Carmel rises abruptly from the sea.
hence the chain of Carmel runs S.S.E. for some 20 miles,
ividing the Coastal Plain from the Plain of Esdraelon. About
Dothan and Tul Keran it merges in the range comprising
he mountains of Samaria and Judæa, which range runs north
nd south through the land like the backbone of a fish, with
teep spurs, like ribs, thrown out on either side towards the
Coastal Plain and the Jordan Valley. Westwards, we look
own upon the cultivated plain, and across it to the golden
elt of sand dunes, tapering like the waist of an hour-glass
vhere the olive plain touches the sea at Jaffa; beyond, lies
he deep blue of the Mediterranean. Eastwards is a sheer
byss falling into the Jordan Valley, where that river, like
silver thread, winds its way along until it falls into the
Dead Sea. Beyond, as if across a fifteen-mile moat, rise
bruptly the mountains of Moab. The map of Palestine
uight be aptly compared to a bridge marker. The horizontal
ne is the plain of Esdraelon. In vertical columns " below
ne line " lie the strips of the country which we have just
escribed. " Above the line " are the mountains of Lebanon,
`abor and Hermon, Galilee and the Sea of Tiberias, and the
alleys and rivers of Damascus.

Let us consider these zones in greater detail, more especially
ith regard to their influence on war. The sea, which skirts
`alestine throughout its length, confers a twofold advantage
pon her mistress. In the first place, it provides a supple-
entary line of communication. We have already seen
iat, during the advance across the Desert, sea-borne supplies
om Port Said were landed at El Arish. This method was
ntinued throughout our advance in Palestine, and landing
laces were improvised at various convenient stages. There
no good harbour along this coast; and landing, which has

[1] The point chosen is imaginary. The view described combines
iose obtainable from two or three points in this neighbourhood.

to be done by beach boats, is difficult, especially in a western
wind. Nevertheless, considerable supplies were thus landed
chiefly of fuel and fodder, which would be little liable to
damage by immersion. In the second place, help can be given
during actual military operations by the Navy. Our ships
frequently lay off the coast and bombarded the enemy
positions. Of necessity, each side had a flank resting on the
sea. To the British, this was a feature of strength ; to the
Turk, it was one of weakness. He was compelled therefore
at all times to draw back or " refuse " his coastal flank, while
the British flank was constantly thrown forward menacing
the flank of the enemy.

There is little to be said about the Sand Dunes, though
being on the flank, they were often the scene of operations.
The sand here is soft and the going bad. Recourse in these
operations was therefore had to camel transport. To the
field engineer, difficulties were presented much as in the desert.
During the trench warfare before Gaza, when a raid was
carried out on Beach Post, no attempt was made to cut the
enemy wire with our artillery, but the wire was simply pulled
up by hand with the standards, for which the soft sand had
provided no firm foundations.

The Coastal Plain comprises, towards the north, the Biblical
Plain of Sharon, and, towards the south, the land of Philistia. By this plain, and not through Judæa, lies the road
from the Nile to the Euphrates. Along this plain have marched
the invading armies of all the ages. Though generally a flat
country, the flatness is relieved by a few rolling hills, of no
great height. It is very fertile and has a good supply of
water, contained in wells. It thus presents many advantages
and but few disadvantages, to an army operating in the field.
Roads are good or are easily improvised, while such obstacles
to an invader's advance do not exist here as in the hills. Our
successes in the campaign under consideration were generally attained by first pushing forward along the plain and
then turning right-handed into the hills.

From the plain, the country rises, in places through the intermediate foot hills of the Shephelah, in places more abruptly and directly into the mountains of Judæa. These mountains are of limestone formation, terraced, where possible, for cultivation, and often wooded with olive trees or tilled as corn patches or vineyards. The scenery is rugged and pretty, the hill-sides generally steep, sometimes precipitous. This is the Palestine of the picture books. Deep gorges have been cut out by water action; but, as no rain falls throughout the summer months, these are, for the most part, but dry water-courses. There are a few good springs to be found in the valleys; the villagers upon the hills are, however, mainly dependent upon cisterns constructed in the rock, in which they catch as much water as possible during the winter rains. These mountains formed the stronghold of the Israelites, who never maintained sway for any length of time over the lower surrounding country. The mountains abound in ruins and are rich in caves, such as may have been the Caves of En-gedi and Adullam. One of the caves witnessed a lurid scene in our mountain fighting. A party of the enemy had established themselves in a cave with machine guns. Ghurkhas attacked, and the enemy, after inflicting casualties, thought to make good their escape by a back exit. But outside there were other Ghurkhas lying in wait, and, as the enemy emerged, they killed them all.

We have seen that the general formation of this range of mountains is like the backbone of a fish. We should therefore expect to find communications from north to south easy enough along the "spine" or ridge, but difficult on either side, where there would be a succession of "ribs" or spurs to be crossed. This is the case. There is only one first-class road from north to south through this hill-country, namely, that which runs along the ridge from Samaria through Nablus, Jerusalem, Bethlehem and Hebron to Beersheba. Communications from east to west are, however, more easy along the

spurs and intervening valleys. To attempt an advance north
wards, from spur to spur, is tedious work; after a compara
tively short push a pause is necessary to enable roads to b
constructed for bringing forward guns and supplies. We ha
an illustration of this in March, 1918, when a forward mov
of this character met at first with but moderate oppositior
A pause of a few weeks was necessary to enable fresh road
to be made. In the meantime, the enemy had been heavil
reinforced, and, when the next advance was attempted, stou
resistance was encountered. This hill-country lent itsel
readily to defence. Mutually supporting heights could b
held. A hill, when captured thus, became a focus for fir
concentrated from all the hills around. So when the Turk
attacked us in these hills they met with much less success tha
in the Jordan Valley; and, on the other hand, they wer
able to offer a stouter resistance to our attacks in these hill
than they could on the Coastal Plain.

The Jordan Valley, as we have already seen, is more than
thousand feet below the level of the Mediterranean, that is
below what we speak of as "sea level." In this respect i
is unique in the geography of the world. In winter tim
the climate is equable; in summer it is unbearable. In peac
time, even the Bedouin forsake it in summer. The distric
is pestilential to a degree, and, in no sense of the word, a whit
man's country. It possesses a feature of considerable import
ance in the river Jordan itself, almost the only river in Pales
tine with a perennial flow. The river is tortuous and rapid
and not adapted to navigation. These features indicate thi
area as a difficult one in which to hold a fighting line, and a
no less difficult one across which to maintain communications
In the summer of 1918, our line ran along the river valley
and the troops in this sector suffered much from diseases.

East of this strong natural boundary formed by the deep
trough of the Jordan, we find a very different country. I
rises abruptly from the Jordan Valley, and is in itself a plateau

It is at first fertile, but, at distances ranging from 40 to 60 miles inland, it merges into steppe and then into sheer desert. Thus it is a country apart, difficult of access from Jerusalem and Western Palestine, more easy of access from Damascus or from Arabia. Through it, from north to south, runs the Hejaz railway, on its way from Damascus to Medina. And so it proved an area in which the Turks, based on Damascus, and the Arabs, operating from Hejaz, were at greater advantage than our columns based on Jerusalem.

We have now glanced at those portions of Palestine in which took place the principal fighting in this campaign. Our review would still be incomplete if we omitted all reference to the Plain of Esdraelon. Starting from the sea coast immediately north of Cape Carmel, at the ports of Haifa and Acre, this Plain runs east south-east across the country to the Jordan Valley. Rising slightly at first, it forms the watershed of "that ancient river, the river Kishon." After the watershed is crossed, there is a drop towards the Jordan Valley; this latter portion of the Plain constitutes the Vale of Jezreel. This Plain of Esdraelon is Armageddon. Here Barak overthrew Sisera, Gideon defeated the Midianites, and Saul and Jonathan met disaster and death at the hands of the Philistines. Here Josiah was defeated and slain by Pharaoh Necho. Near here, the Christians were defeated and their kingdom overthrown by the Saracens. On this Plain Napoleon won his final and crushing victory over the Turks.

No battle, beyond a few cavalry engagements, took place here during the campaign which we are to consider. The Turks had been totally defeated before ever this line was reached. But this Plain has still for us a military interest. It may well be that here, where the mountains of Samaria overlook and command all approaches from the north, is to be found the best strategic line for the defence of the Suez Canal.

In a country like Palestine, where levels and characteristics

are so divergent, diversities of climate are to be expected.
We have seen that the summer climate of the Lower Jordan
Valley is pestilential. Parts of the Coastal Plain also are
very malarious, particularly from north of Jaffa to Mount
Carmel. With these exceptions, the climate is by no means
unpleasant nor unsuitable for the conduct of military operations. Far enough south to enjoy plenty of bright sunshine
it is still some distance north of the tropics. Pleasant and
regular breezes from the sea mitigate the discomfort which
might otherwise prevail in a country almost surrounded by
desert. The whole of the rainfall comes in the winter months.
From about April to October, though dews are heavy, rain is
unknown. But in the winter months, especially December
and January, and to some extent February, the rainfall is
intense, and the country on the Plains and lower lying districts
is reduced to a sea of mud well-nigh impassable. Thus military operations in summer are liable to be prejudiced by a
shortage of water; in winter by an excess. The ideal season
for operations is therefore in the spring, when there is an
abundance of water and a plentiful feed; and, next to this, the
autumn, when the heat of the summer has passed its height and
the rains of winter have not yet made the country impassable.

The importance of good railways in modern war is immense.
We have already traced the construction of the broad gauge
line from Egypt which followed close behind the British in
their advance across the Desert and into Southern Palestine.
The Turks in Western Palestine were at a perpetual disadvantage through the inferiority of the railway service;
but, in Eastern Palestine, i.e. across the Jordan, the position
was reversed. Before the war, Syria had been connected
with Asia Minor by a broad gauge line from Aleppo to Rayak
where it effected a junction with a narrow gauge line from
Beyrout to Damascus. The broad gauge line was part of
the Baghdad railway scheme. But at this time, that railway
even between Constantinople and Aleppo, was only partially

completed. The tunnelling of the Taurus Mountains was
yet unfinished. Thus troops or supplies, coming from Constantinople to Damascus, had to break the journey at the
Taurus Mountains and again at Rayak. These two interrup-
tions provided admirable opportunities for delay and confusion, which the dilatory Turk embraced. The tunnelling
of the Taurus was pushed on with during the war, and in 1918
rumours reached us that these mountains had been pierced,
so that trains could then run through from Constantinople
(Haida Pasha) to Rayak. The installation of more business-
like Germans at the latter station went far towards minimis-
ing the delays and confusion due to the break of gauge.

From Damascus, the Hejaz railway, constructed nominally
for Mecca pilgrims, runs due south, and, passing along the high
plateau of Eastern Palestine, had already reached Medina.
A branch from this line, starting from a junction at Deraa,
ran westwards along the Plain of Esdraelon to Haifa. Another
line, almost parallel to the Hejaz railway, ran from Damascus
due south to Mezerib ; this line was removed by the Turks
after the commencement of the war, as the materials were
required for railway construction elsewhere. Unconnected
with any of these railways, a French line ran from Jaffa to
Jerusalem ; this also the Turks removed, as between Jaffa
and Ludd, while, for the remainder of its length, they altered
the gauge so as to adapt it to the rolling stock of the Hejaz
Railway. All these railways south of Damascus were narrow-
gauge lines, without much rolling stock available, so that
their carrying capacity was limited.

On the outbreak of war, the Turks, acting under the guidance
of the Germans, embarked upon a considerable programme
of railway construction. Starting from a point on the Plain
of Esdraelon, El Apele, they constructed a new line which
crossed the mountains about Samaria and reached the Plain
of Sharon at Tul Keram. Thence it ran down the length of
the Coastal Plain to Beersheba, and, ultimately, to Auja in

the Desert. This railway was constructed in 1915 for t
invasion of Egypt. Into this railway was incorporated po
tions of the old Jaffa-Jerusalem line, as between Ludd a
"Junction Station." This was the none too distincti
name given to the important station which was construct
at the point where the older railway left the Plain ; this n
became the junction for Jerusalem. At a later date, the Tur
withdrew from Auja to Beersheba, the line south of the latt
place was removed and a new line was constructed from ne
Junction Station to points just north of Gaza.

Roads in the coastal sector are good, though difficult i
heavy motor traffic after rain. In the hills the only firs
class roads were the road running north and south along t'
ridge from Nablus through Jerusalem to Beersheba, and t
road west and east from Jaffa to Jerusalem, continued eas
wards through Jericho and across the Jordan to Es Salt an
Amman Station on the Hejaz Railway.

The population of Palestine is very mixed, comprisi
Moslems, Christians and Jews with their various subdivisio
and sects. The Moslem inhabitants, Arabs and Syrian
have little in common with the Turks except their religio
The Jews and the Christians groaned under Turkish oppre
sion. Both Jews and Christians welcomed the advent of t
British, while the Moslems accepted the situation, if not wi
pleasure, at least with equanimity. The Turks themselv
form no part of the regular population. They are alien rule
speaking a language unknown to the people, and incapa
of understanding the language of the country. Althou
Palestine has been governed by Moslems for upwards of
thousand years, it has only been annexed to the Ottom
Empire for four centuries. More than once during that peri
it would have been torn away but for the aid of the Britis
The government of Syria by the Ottoman Turk had been oppre
sive and corrupt and marked by the discouragement of
progress and enterprise. It was high time that it should ceas

CHAPTER V

GAZA

GAZA! What pictures this name conjures up in our imagination. From childhood the city has been familiar to us for its dramatic associations with Samson. It was here that he removed the city gates and carried them to the summit of Ali Muntar, " to the top of an hill that is before Hebron," and it was here that he took hold of the two middle pillars, and, bowing himself with all his might, destroyed the temple of Dagon with the thousands of Philistines that were his tormentors. The whole history of Gaza is steeped in blood. It is the outpost of Africa, the gate of Asia. Throughout the ages its strategic importance has been immense. Scarcely an invading army has passed here without fighting a battle. It figured in the wars of the Eastern invaders, was totally destroyed by Alexander the Great, was the scene of one of Napoleon's battles, and, during our campaign, saw six months of trench warfare and no less than three distinct and sanguinary engagements. In the course of its history, Gaza is said to have been taken and destroyed in war between forty and fifty times. No city in the world has been destroyed more often. Happy, indeed is the city that has no history !

Prior to this war, Gaza was a town of some 40,000 inhabitants, mostly Moslems, to whom the city is sacred. It owed its importance in modern times to being the junction of the caravan routes from Egypt to Syria and from Arabia to the Mediterranean. The town itself stands back some couple of miles from the sea, from which it is separated by sand dunes.

57

It is surrounded by gardens and plantations ; most of th
are bordered by thick cactus hedges, which played a pro:
nent part in the days of trench warfare. The surround
country is by no means level, but consists of rolling ara
land with low ridges and some hills. The most promin-
feature is the hill, Ali Muntar, a commanding height sou
east of the town. When we first approached it, the hill \
clad with trees and surrounded by a tomb ; but six mont
persistent bombardment soon removed the trees and to:
and altered the conformation of the hill. There are ot
ridges lying about the town, which were afterwards inc
porated in the defensive schemes of the Turks and of ourselv
The geographical feature of principal military importa:
in this neighbourhood is the Wadi Ghuzzeh. This wadi
a watercourse, which, in times of rain, carries off the wa
from the hills between Beersheba and the Dead Sea. It ru
approximately, from south-east to north-west, at right ang
to the coast line, and passes Gaza at a distance of about 4 mi
from the south-western or Egyptian side of the town. Duri
the greater part of the year this watercourse is dry, thou
the sides are steep, and wheeled traffic can only cross at prope
constructed crossings. On either side of this wadi, dista
a mile or so from its bed, are ridges which run approximat
parallel to the wadi. That on the right bank is known
Mansura Ridge, that on the left bank as In Seirat. I
latter is a relatively high ridge and affords cover for troc
beyond. On the other side of this ridge, protected by
and distant some nine or ten miles from Gaza, is a sm
village with a good supply of water. This village is kno
as Deir el Belah, or, more frequently, merely as Belah.
formed our advanced base during the later operations agai:
Gaza.

We have seen that, at the end of February, 1917, Gene
Dobell's force had reached El Arish, while portions of it b
crossed the border at Rafa, and his cavalry had occup:

Khan Yunus. The Turks had withdrawn to Gaza, where they now took up a position. They had one force at Gaza and another in the neighbourhood of Beersheba, with other troops between. In March, it was decided to attack the enemy at Gaza. The British force was concentrated at Rafa, whence it marched up secretly by night. On the night of the 25th March, it moved forward from Belah against the first objective, the In Seirat Ridge. This was secured without serious opposition. There was a dense fog on the morning of the 26th, and, as the troops were moving through standing crops, finding the way was none too easy. However, the Wadi Ghuzzeh was crossed, and the high ground at Mansura Ridge was secured. From there, an attack was delivered across the open against Ali Muntar and Gaza. The main attack was made by the 53rd Division, plus one Brigade of the the 54th, while the 52nd Division were in reserve. Our troops captured, and established themselves on Ali Muntar, and also on the hill beyond, known as Australia Hill. From these points they looked down upon and dominated the town of Gaza. Meanwhile, the cavalry had been ordered to go round by the right, and to cut off the enemy when he should retreat. The cavalry not only got round, but succeeded in entering the town itself, where they captured some of the Turkish staff. The Turks believed that the game was up, and were now preparing to surrender. It was the opinion of many who took part in the battle, that, had we held on for a short time longer, we should have captured the town and the whole of this force, and that we should have then been in a position to meet and to defeat the enemy reinforcements, since the 52nd Division in reserve had not yet been brought into action. However, Turkish reinforcements were now reported to be coming up from the direction of Beersheba, and to be threatening our right flank. Accordingly, a withdrawal was ordered, and our troops fell back on the Mansura Ridge, the New Zealanders coming right through the town of Gaza itself. That

night, orders were given for an immediate retirement, an
our forces recrossed the Wadi Ghuzzeh. The bulk of th
force retired to Belah, while outposts held the In Seirat Ridg
After a two days' battle, wherein complete success had bee
almost within our grasp, we had but little to show save casua
ties.

From the summit of In Seirat Ridge, a commanding vie
is obtained over the whole country from Gaza to Beersheb;
From this point of vantage the Turks could be seen, througl
out the first fortnight in April, busily digging themselves
and wiring their positions. We, on our side, were no le;
assiduous in preparations for another battle. Patrols wer
sent out to reconnoitre the country, and working parties wer
out into No Man's Land to construct ramparts and make a
preparations for getting guns across the Wadi Ghuzzeh. Th
74th Division were brought up to Belah. A few of the newl
invented "tanks" arrived from England, and aroused grea
expectations.

The day of the second battle of Gaza arrived. On the 16t
April, the force moved out from Belah and crossed the Wac
Ghuzzeh by night. On this occasion, the first objective wa
Mansura Ridge, which was captured without much difficult;
The second, and principal objective, was the strong line c
Turkish positions to the south and south-east of Gaza, an
fronting the Gaza—Beersheba road. The troops detailed fo
the attack were the 52nd, the 53rd and the 54th Division;
the 54th to move forward from Mansura, the 52nd on thei
left and the 53rd close to the sea. It was contemplated tha
most of our difficulties would be obviated by a long artiller
preparation and by the newly arrived tanks which had acquire
a high reputation in France. Accordingly, the enemy pos
tions were shelled for two hours, and then the infantr
advanced, preceded by these tanks. But, alas, the tank;
were few in number; some were soon put out of action, c
caught fire; and the hopes that they had raised were di

ppointed. The infantry advanced over some 3,000 yards of perfectly open plain, until they reached the enemy's uncut wire; here they were mown down by the enemy's machine guns. That night, those that were able to do so, crept back under cover of darkness to Mansura Ridge. The dead lay where they fell, a gruesome spectacle, for over six months, until buried by our own parties after the third battle of Gaza. Those that returned were collected and reorganized at Mansura Ridge, and at once commenced to dig in at this position. This was the night of the 19th April. Next morning, the Turks came pouring out of their positions to gloat over their success. By this time we had done little more than scratch the surface; had the Turks closed to deliver a determined counter-attack, they might have made matters distinctly uncomfortable. As it was, they came out merely as spectators. Our guns opened upon them and they withdrew. After this, our digging proceeded apace, and we soon had a satisfactory position entrenched from Mansura to the sea.

There is a saying in the East that the British always come back, meaning that reverses only make them more determined to try again and to succeed. Thus did the British come back into the Soudan, and into the Transvaal. Thus was the surrender of Kut wiped out by the capture of Baghdad. And so were our losses at Gaza in this spring avenged by our victory on these same battlefields in the following autumn. For the time being, however, both sides settled down to the routine life of modern trench warfare.

Now followed a complete reorganization of our army in Egypt. On the 28th June, 1917, the post of Commander-in-Chief of the Egyptian Expeditionary Force was taken over by General Sir Edmund Allenby, G.C.M.G., K.C.B. The organization into an Eastern Force under a subordinate commander, which had been instituted in the summer of 1916, was abolished, and the force was organized in Corps. The strength of the Egyptian Expeditionary Force was augmented,

much artillery being added, besides three divisions of infantr
The 10th (Irish) and the 60th (London) Divisions were broug
across from Salonica. The 75th Division was organized
the country and consisted of four battalions of Indian troop
taken from the Suez Canal Zone defences, and nine battalio
of West of England Territorials, that had been in the Ea
since the beginning of the war, and had, for the most pai
been garrisoning India.

When this reorganization was complete, this army w.
constituted as follows : The 20th Corps, comprising the 10
(Irish), the 53rd (Welsh), the 60th (London) and the 74
(Dismounted Yeomanry) Divisions. The 21st Corps, compri
ing the 52nd (Scottish Lowland), the 54th (East Anglia
and the 75th (Wessex and Indian) Divisions. The Dese
Mounted Corps, comprising the Australian Mounted Divisio
the Anzac Mounted Division and the Yeomanry Divisio
General Allenby had, as his Chief-of-Staff, Major-Gener
L. J. Bols, C.B., D.S.O. In addition to the above troop
there was, on this front, a composite brigade, consisting
French and Italians, familiarly known as the " Mixed Ve
mouth " Brigade. Other regiments were represented, suc
as Indian Imperial troops, and battalions of the British We
India Regiment, while representative units of the Egyptia
Army did duty upon the Lines of Communication.

Although each Division was associated with some particula
portion of Great Britain, from which it took its name, th
association was not exclusive. Thus, the 52nd Lowlan
Division had at least one Highland Battalion, the 53rd Wel
had more battalions from England than from Wales, and th
54th East Anglian contained one battalion from London an
one from the South of England. It will be best, therefor
if, in our future pages, we refer to divisions only by numbe

An interesting feature about General Allenby's army wa
that, from this time forward, the greater portion consisted
Territorials.

CHAPTER VI

TRENCH WARFARE

T was in the late summer of 1917 that the regiment with
    which I was serving joined the Expeditionary Force.
ming from India, we landed at Suez and were railed through
once to Kantara. This place we found a hive of industry,
befitted the military base of so important an expedition.
ke other units similarly arriving from India, we were kept
re for a fortnight. This time was devoted to the equipping
the battalion on the scale applicable to this country, with
insport, draught and riding animals, Lewis guns and such
her equipment as we required for the operations on which
were to embark.

immediately we were ready to move, we were railed up to
e Front, to Belah, which, at that time, was railhead. This
is our first experience of travelling on the Kantara Military
ilway, and is not likely to be forgotten. The shortage of
lling stock available did not permit of troops, or, at that
ne, even of officers accompanying troops, travelling in pas-
nger coaches. On the contrary, a number of open trucks
re adapted for troop traffic, being roofed over with a cover-
g affording protection from the sun but with sides left open.
ese trucks had neither continuous brakes nor screw coup-
gs. Our journey, therefore, was enlivened by the fre-
ent successful attempts of our truck to overtake the truck
ead, followed by a difference of opinion with the truck
hind, a wavering between two opinions, and then another
ad plunge into the darkness in pursuit of the truck ahead,

43

and the next check brought about a repetition of this pleasi
diversion from sleep. If the writer of a recent popular so
really believed that the Sands of the Desert never grow col
let him try travelling across them by night in an open truc
The train was not furnished with that luxury of modern trav
steam heating. For the men, a substitute was found k
adopting the method by which sheep are kept cosy on simil
occasions, that is, by packing into each truck a few more th:
it can accommodate. The officers rolled themselves up
their valises, bruised every protruding bone in their bodi
"and wished for the day."

On arrival at the Front, we moved first into a position
reserve near the Wadi Ghuzzeh. As we crossed the summ
of In Seirat Ridge, what a view unfolded itself before o
eyes! Before us lay the Plain of Philistia, spreading fro
the sea to the Judæan Hills, to our left front lay the whi
buildings of the town of Gaza, while, ever and anon, we
heard and seen the booming of cannon and the bursting of she

We were now put through a gradual process of acclimatiz
tion. Ensconced in one of the offshoots of the Wadi Ghuzze
well behind the front line, we enjoyed safety from shellin
We were, however, sufficiently in the picture to have gun
constantly firing around us and aeroplanes flying overhea
and could watch our friends being shelled in the front line ar
the daily anti-aeroplane shoots, both by our own and by th
enemy's "Archies." Here we were able to carry out a certai
amount of training, and to organize the battalion upon th
lines of the new "normal formation," giving the platoo
commander control over each kind of weapon with which th
infantry are armed—rifle, bayonet, bomb, rifle-bomb an
Lewis gun. Gas masks were issued, and all ranks were in
structed in their use. In a couple of weeks this training, o
rather adaptation of our previous training to the condition
of trench warfare upon this front, had so far progressed th:
we could enter upon the next stage of our acclimatizatio

ndividual companies were now sent up into the front line for instruction." This consisted of their being attached o other units that were garrisoning the front line. Our men ere posted in the trenches with men of such other units; nd some of the officers and men accompanied patrols into No Man's Land." After three weeks of acclimatization, e moved up to the front line and ourselves took over a secon of the defences. And here we remained until after the all of Gaza.

The Turkish army at this time, as we have seen, held a rong position from the sea at Gaza, roughly along the main aza—Beersheba road to Beersheba. His force was on a ide front, the distance from Gaza to Beersheba being about miles. Gaza itself had been made into a strong modern rtress, heavily entrenched and wired, offering every facility r protracted defence. The civilian population had been acuated. The remainder of the enemy's line consisted iginally of a series of strong localities, which were known as e Sihan group of works, the Atawinah group, the Baha oup, the Abu Hareira—Arab el Teeaha trench system, and ally, the works covering Beersheba. During the period om July to October, the defences had been considerably rengthened, and these strong localities had, by the end of ctober, been joined up to form a practically continuous line om the sea to a point south of Sheria, except for a gap of me 1,500 to 2,000 yards between Ali Muntar and the Sihan oup. The defensive works round Beersheba remained a tached system, but had been improved and extended. A w railway had been made from El Tine, just south of Juncn Station on the Damascus-Beersheba railway to Beit anun, just north of Gaza, with a subsidiary branch to Huj, e latter intended to supply the centre of the defensive line. was evident, therefore, that the enemy was determined to ake every effort to maintain his position on the Gaza-ersheba line.

The British force was extended on a front of 22 miles from the sea opposite Gaza to Gamli. About 6 miles inland, the Wadi Ghuzzeh is joined by a short tributary wadi, on the right bank, known as the Wadi Nukhabir. The point at which this wadi commenced was about a mile or so nearer to the enemy than the line of our positions opposite Gaza. Its head-waters (to use an expression scarcely appropriate to a dry watercourse) were within the apex of a V-shaped escarpment, the point of the V protruding towards the enemy. The feature might be compared to a heel-mark in soft ground. On the convex side were slight ridges with gentle forward slopes ; on the concave were steep escarpments. The ridges of the V were known as Mansura and Sheikh Abbas Ridges respectively ; the point was merely known as " The Apex." Our trench system here ran along the forward slopes of these ridges, a hundred yards or so below the crest, whence the country fell towards the enemy in a gentle glacis slope devoid of cover. Our reserves and our day positions were behind the escarpment, where was excellent cover from hostile shelling. The portion of the enemy's works in front of this sector was the Sihan group, a strongly prepared position distant about a mile. The apex itself formed a salient, necessary to hold since its Ridges would otherwise have dominated our positions ; but, though a salient, the position was undoubtedly strong. The situation and the conformation of the Apex therefore, both invited attack and assisted defence. From the sea to the Apex we had a continuous line of trenches. Beyond Sheikh Abbas our defences consisted of a series of redoubts, our right flank being to some extent in the air. Here, however, was a waterless desert, so difficult to cross that this flank could be sufficiently protected by cavalry patrols.

Considering that there was a war on, campaigning life on this front was by no means uncomfortable. Those who had seen service in France bemoaned the lack of comforts and

amusements behind the line, and the absence of home leave,
those who had come from Salonica were congratulating themselves on the exchange ; while those of us who had been in
Mesopotamia during the bad times of 1916, considered ourselves in the lap of luxury. Rations were good and plentiful
and canteen well stocked. The Turkish rations, on the other
hand, were scanty and poor, with the result that morale was
low, discomfort rife, and desertions frequent. On one occasion, when the enemy were making a raid upon our trenches,
a couple of Turks got into an empty bag where one of our
men had left his pack. The manner in which they pursued
their advantage was by helping themselves to his tin of bully
beef and getting away with all speed. A Turkish officer, who
was subsequently taken prisoner, said, " If the Turkish rations
had been as good as yours, you would never have captured
Gaza."

The health of our troops, on the whole, was good. In so far
as there was sickness it consisted of a certain amount of
dysentery, almost unavoidable in an army in the Field, septic
sores, which are unusually rife, and a slight epidemic of sand-
fly fever. Foremost among the inconveniences to be toler-
ated were the flies, which made it difficult for the men to sleep
by day, the time when they most need rest after manning the
trenches all night. Next to the flies came the dust. The
country, in which for the time we were making our home,
consisted of arable ground devoid of crops, and thoroughly
cut up by the passing of transport. A breeze, that blew daily
without fail, served to raise a fine impalpable dust that per-
meated everything. This powder dust made marching difficult, but wise forethought caused galvanized iron netting to
be laid along all the principal routes, forming " wire roads "
for the use of light motor-cars and " foot-sloggers." If we
grumbled at the dust, we had, at this time at least, no cause
to complain, like our brethren in Flanders, of the mud. Taken
all together, the morale was good and the men distinctly happy.

Life in these days was not without its diversions and touches of humour. A nice Roman tessellated pavement was unearthed near the Wadi Ghuzzeh, at the place called Umm Jerar, which is associated with Abraham. Going one day to look for it, I found a military policeman on duty within half a mile of the spot. I said to him, " Can you tell me the way to the tessellated pavement ? " He looked at me vacantly for a minute and then replied : " Is it the wire road that you happen to mean, sir ? " On one occasion, the General was going round the front line accompanied by the Intelligence Officer (who is the Officer that selects the pass-word which is changed daily) and by the C.O. of the unit in this sector. Staying out rather later than they had intended, it was dusk or dark when they approached one of the posts. The sentry challenged, " Halt—hands up." Up went the General's hands in prompt compliance. " Advance one, and give the counter-sign," continued the sentry. The General turned to the Intelligence Officer, " What is the countersign to-day ? " said he. " Really I am afraid I have forgotten," replied the Intelligence Officer, and both referred to the Colonel. " When I left my headquarters, it had not yet come through," was his reply. The sentry remained obdurate. Then followed explanations, and, after some parley and identifications, the party were allowed to proceed. As they were leaving, the General hurried again to the sentry, saying, " Well, my man, you might just tell us now what the pass-word is." " I am sorry, sir," was his reply, " but I haven't the least idea."

About this time the spy peril was rather rife. We had orders not to leave our lines without revolvers, for protection against assassination by spies. To one particular " hush-hush " spot rode up a General with his Staff Officer, both faultlessly attired, accompanied by the usual Orderly. The General asked to be shown round, and his request was conceded with the thoroughness and courtesy due to his high rank. His inspection completed, the General expressed his

hanks, and the party rode away, never to be heard of again,—
t least not in that capacity. Shortly afterwards, a notorious
py was seen working as a coolie in the Egyptian Labour
Corps. Perhaps he was the General.

The monotony of trench life was varied by occasional
aids into the enemy trenches. Some very successful raids
were carried out on the enemy's defences near the sea, especi-
lly at Beach Post, and other successful raids were made from
he Apex upon the advanced trenches of the Sihan group of
vorks. Mutual bombardments frequently enlivened the
roceedings, the supremacy in which undoubtedly lay with
ur artillery. These never allowed a day to pass without
oing some firing, and they had sniping guns ever ready to
re on any movement that might be seen in enemy territory.
he enemy guns, largely manned by Austrians, reserved their
re for concentrated bombardments; evidently they were
ess able to replenish their supplies of ammunition.

The sector of the front line which fell to our lot to hold
vas a portion of the Apex. Our front line companies manned
 continuous system of trenches, while the reserve company
nd headquarters occupied dug-outs dug into, or constructed
ith sand bags upon, the steep slopes of the escarpment.
here were deep tunnel dug-outs, extending into the bowels
f the earth, in the support area, but these were never used.
n the front line there were no such dug-outs, except for such
urposes as signal office and platoon head-quarters. In
ise of intense shelling, the front line garrison, except sentries,
uld obtain fair cover behind the traverses in the narrow
enches which connected up the wider and more exposed fire
ays. It is a debatable question whether deep dug-outs
 or near the front line are advisable. When the enemy
iells intensively, if he means business, his barrage is closely
llowed by his infantry. When the barrage lifts, therefore,
 is of vital importance to man the fire-step immediately.
 is not easy to turn a large number of men quickly out of

deep dug-outs which may thus prove only a Fool's Paradis
In one of the raids made near the sea, our infantry, followin
closely up to the barrage, caught the enemy taking refu
in dug-outs, and had no difficulty in capturing or accountir
for the whole garrison of the raided trench. At the Ap
we were three times bombarded and raided. On each occ
sion the garrison merely took refuge behind the traverse
Although they endured it, the bombardment was much mo
uncomfortable here than if the men had been in good dug-out:
yet they were able to man the trenches so quickly that in r
case could the enemy effect a lodgment, and in only one ca
did he even reach the trench.

When we took over the Apex, the days of sporadic raids k
us were past, and all thought was concentrated on prepar
tions for the great day that was then imminent. On ti
other hand, there was great patrolling activity. Our officer
patrols went out nightly into No Man's Land, and brougl
back information as to enemy works in progress and activil
in their trenches. These patrols had many exciting exper
ences, and, in the dark, frequently encountered patrols se
out by the enemy. Much useful information was brought
by these patrols to the battalions holding this sector of tl
line, especially during the first few days after the commenc
ment of the great offensive which resulted in the capture
Gaza and Beersheba.

SKETCH MAP

OF COUNTRY ROUND GAZA
AND BEERSHEBA

ILLUSTRATING OPERATIONS FROM
MARCH TO NOVEMBER 1917

TO HEBRON
15 MILES

o TOWAL
ABU JERWAL

o MUWEILEH

EL SHEBA

NUKAH

IRGEIG

BEERSHEBA

GIRHEIR

TO AUJA
40. MLS

(1070)
S H

KARM

BUGGAR

ESANA

KHALASA

10 MILES

50,000

TO AUJA
20 MILES

CHAPTER VII

GAZA AND BEERSHEBA

THE plan by which General Allenby defeated the Turks and captured their Gaza—Beersheba line, involved three distinct operations. It will be remembered that the enemy defences consisted of a substantially continuous line from the sea at Gaza to Arab el Teeaha, where the left flank was bent back or "refused" at or about Sheria. Some 4½ miles farther on were the detached works covering Beersheba, which thus constituted a strong outwork protecting the left flank of the main position. The decisive blow was to be struck against the left flank of the main Turkish position at Hareira and Sheria. Before this blow could be struck, it was necessary to clear away the obstacle presented by Beersheba. It was also necessary to keep the enemy in doubt as to where the decisive blow was to fall, so another operation, on as large a scale as the available force would permit, and calculated both to mystify the enemy and to draw off a portion of his reserves, was undertaken on the immediate sea front at Gaza. Thus we get, firstly, the capture of Beersheba ; secondly, the attack on the Gaza coastal defences ; and, thirdly, the main attack delivered against Sheria.

" This plan of operations was chosen for the following reasons. The enemy's works in the Hareira-Sheria sector were less formidable than elsewhere, and they were easier of approach than other parts of the enemy's defences. The capture of Beersheba was a necessary preliminary to the main operation, in order to secure the water supply at that place,

and to give room for the deployment of the attacking force
the high ground to the north and north-west of Beershel
from which direction the main attack was to be develope
When Beersheba was in our hands, we should have an op
flank against which to operate, and full use could be made
our superiority in mounted troops. Moreover, a success he
offered prospects of pursuing our advantage, and forcing t
enemy to abandon the rest of his fortified positions, whi
no other line of attack would afford."

The difficulties to be overcome in the operations again
Beersheba and the Hareira-Sheria line were considerab
Foremost among them were our old friend, the shortage
water, and, scarcely less formidable, the difficulty of transpor

With regard to water, no supply existed in the area ov
which operations were to take place. "An ample suppl
of water was known to exist at Beersheba, but it was unce
tain how quickly it could be developed or to what exter
the enemy would have damaged the wells before we succeede
in occupying the town. Except at Beersheba, no large suppl
of water would be found till Sheria and Hareira had been ca
tured. Arrangements had therefore to be made to ensu
that the troops could be kept supplied with water, whi
operating at considerable distances from their original wate
base, for a period which might amount to a week or more.
This was to some extent met by developing the water suppli
at Ecani, Khalassa and Asluj, all places in No Man's Lan
some miles beyond our right flank.

The transport problem was no less difficult. Beersheb
itself some thousand feet above the sea level, lies in a rece
on the western slopes of the Judæan Hills. In the bed
this recess runs the Wadi Es Saba. Towards the north-ea
a good metalled road leads gradually to the summit of th
hills and on through Hebron to Jerusalem. North-west
good road led along the enemy's front to Gaza. Th
railway line, avoiding the heights, for the first ten or twelv

miles follows approximately the direction of the Gaza road, and then turns northwards along the Plain or Foothills. But south of the Gaza-Beersheba line there were no good roads, " and no reliance could therefore be placed on the use of motor transport." Owing to the steep banks of many of the wadis which intersected the area of operations, the routes passable by wheeled transport were limited, and, in many places, the going was heavy and difficult.

Practically the whole of the transport available in the force, including 30,000 pack camels, had to be allotted to one portion of the eastern force, to enable it to be kept supplied with food, water and ammunition, at a distance of 15 to 20 miles in advance of railhead.

There already existed a branch from the Kantara military railway; which branch, leaving the main line at Rafa, ran to Shellal and Gamli, supplying the right of our line. Arrangements were made for this railhead to be pushed forward as rapidly as possible from Shellal towards Karm (some 7 miles to the east-south-east of Shellal), and for a line to be laid from Gamli towards Beersheba for the transport of ammunition. No Man's Land being some 10 or 12 miles wide in this sector, railway construction was carried on in front of our front line under cover of yeomanry outposts.

This line of outposts was attacked on the morning of the 27th October by a strong reconnoitring party that the Turks sent out from the direction of Kauwukah to make a reconnaissance towards Karm. On a Division of our infantry coming up, the Turks withdrew.

By the end of October all our preparations were ready. The bombardment of the Gaza defences commenced on the 27th and continued nightly. On the 30th, warships of the Royal Navy, assisted by a French battleship, began co-operating in this bombardment. The actual infantry attack on Gaza was not intended to take place, however, until after the capture of Beersheba, and was delayed accordingly.

The date fixed for the attack on Beersheba was the 31st October. The plan was to attack with two divisions the hostile works between the Khalassa Road and the Wadi Saba, that is, the sector to the south-west of the town. The works north of the Wadi Saba were to be masked with the Imperial Camel Corps and some infantry, while a portion of the 53rd Division further north covered the left of the Corps. The right of the attack was covered by a cavalry regiment. Further east, mounted troops took up a line opposite the southern defences of Beersheba. A mounted force, starting from Khalassa and Asluj, beyond our original right flank, were detailed to make a wide flanking movement and attack Beersheba from the east and north-east.

The units detailed for the attack moved by a night march and were in their appointed positions by dawn of the 31st. As a preliminary to the main attack, in order to enable field guns to be brought within effective range for wire-cutting an attack was made upon the enemy's advanced works on the high ground about a couple of miles south-west of the town at Hill 1070. This had been successfully accomplished by 8.45 a.m., and the cutting of the wire proceeded satisfactorily though pauses had to be made to allow the dust to clear. The assault was ordered for 12.15 p.m., and proved successful. By about 10 p.m., the whole of the works between the Khalassa Road and the Wadi Saba were in our hands.

" Meanwhile the mounted troops, after a night march of for a portion of the force, some 35 miles, arrived early on the same morning, the 31st, at about Khasim Zanna, in the hills some 5 miles east of Beersheba. From the hills, the advance into Beersheba from the east and north-east lies over an open and almost flat plain, commanded by the rising ground north of the town and flanked by an underfeature in the Wadi Saba, called Tel el Saba.

" A force was sent north to secure Bir es Sakaly, on the Hebron Road, and protect the right flank. This force

t with some opposition, and was engaged with hostile
valry at Bir es Sakaly and to the north during the day.
l el Saba was found strongly held by the enemy, and was
t captured till late in the afternoon.

" Meanwhile, attempts to advance in small parties across
e plain towards the town made slow progress. In the
ening, however, a mounted attack by Australian Light
orse, who rode straight at the town from the East, proved
mpletely successful. They galloped over two deep trenches
ld by the enemy just outside the town, and entered the
wn at about 7 p.m., capturing numerous prisoners.

" A very strong position was thus taken with slight loss,
d the Turkish detachment at Beersheba almost completely
t out of action. This success laid open the left flank of
e main Turkish position for a decisive blow."

The actual date of the attack at Gaza had been left open
l the result of the attack at Beersheba was known, as it was
ended that the attack on Gaza, which was designed to draw
stile reserves towards that sector, should take place a day
two before the attack on the Sheria position. After the
mplete success of the Beersheba operations, it was decided
at the attack on Gaza should take place on the morning of
e 2nd November.

" The objectives of this attack were the hostile works from
nbrella Hill (2,000 yards south-west of the town) to Sheikh
isan, on the sea (about 2,500 yards north-west of the town).
ie front of the attack was about 6,000 yards, and Sheikh
isan, the farthest objective, was over 3,000 yards from our
nt line. The ground over which the attack took place
nsisted of sand dunes, rising in places up to 150 feet in
ight. This sand is very deep and heavy going. The enemy's
fences consisted of several lines of strongly built trenches
d redoubts.

" As Umbrella Hill flanked the advance against the Turkish
rks farther west, it was decided to capture it by a prelimin-

ary operation, to take place four hours previous to the main attack. It was accordingly attacked and captured at 11. p.m. on the 1st November by a portion of the 52nd Division This attack drew a heavy bombardment of Umbrella Hill itself and our front lines, which lasted for two hours, bu ceased in time to allow the main attack, which was timed for 3.0 a.m., to form up without interference."

This attack partook of the nature of a modern trench to trench advance, as seen on the battlefields of France, with the co-operation of tanks and the accompaniment of other pro ducts of modern science. It was successful in reaching most of its objectives. The enemy losses were heavy, especially from the preliminary bombardment.

" Subsequent reports from prisoners stated that one of the Divisions holding the Gaza Sector was withdrawn on accoun of casualties, a Division from the general reserve being drawn into this Sector to replace it. The attack thus succeeded in its primary object, which was to prevent any units being withdrawn from the Gaza defences to meet the threat to the Turkish left flank and to draw into Gaza as large a propor tion as possible of the available Turkish reserves. Further the capture of Sheikh Hasan and the south-western defences constituted a very direct threat to the whole of the Gaza position, which could be developed on any sign of a with drawal on the part of the enemy."

Here the force attacking Gaza stayed its hand, merely holding on to the positions already captured, while the main attack was being developed on the right.

Having captured Beersheba on the 31st October, a force was pushed out early on the following day, the 1st November into the hills north of Beersheba, with the object of securing the flank of the attack on Sheria, while mounted troops were sent north along the Hebron road. Accordingly, the 53rd Division took up a position from Towal Abu Jerwal (6 mile north of Beersheba) to Muweileh (3½ miles farther west and

e 10th Division occupied Abu Irgeig, on the railway, 6 miles
om Beersheba.

Next day, the 2nd, our mounted troops found and engaged
nsiderable enemy forces to the north of Towal Abu Jerwal.
ccordingly, on the 3rd, we advanced in that direction towards
n Kohleh and Khuweilfeh, where the enemy were found
 be holding a strong position with considerable and in-
easing forces. It will be borne in mind that this was only
e right flank-guard ; our main attack, which was to be
livered against Sheria, was not timed to commence until
vo or three days later. However, the enemy elected to
mploy the whole of his available reserves in an immediate
unter-attack. During the 4th and 5th he made several
etermined attacks on the mounted troops in this locality.
hese attacks were repulsed ; and the enemy's action was
ot allowed to make any essential modification to the original
an, which it had been decided to carry out at dawn on
ovember 6th. It was this exhausting of the Turkish re-
rves, so early in the operations and so far away to the East
s Khuweilfeh, that paved the way for the success of our
tack on Sheria.

At dawn, on the 6th, the force detailed for the main attack
ad taken up positions of readiness to the south-east of the
auwukah system of trenches. The yeomanry opened the
all by assaulting the group of works forming the extreme
ft of the enemy's defensive system, following this up by an
dvance due west up the railway, capturing the line of
etached works which lay east of the railway line. Mean-
hile, London and Irish troops moved towards the Kauwukah
ystem, bringing forward their guns to within wire-cutting
nge. Soon after noon, these troops commenced their attack
pon the south-eastern face of the Kauwukah system. This
as completely successful in capturing all its objectives.
heria station was also reported as captured before dark. On
is same day the right flank-guard, the 53rd Division, had

successfully attacked Khuweilfeh. The position at nigh
fall, then, was that our right flank-guard were at Kauweilfe
the yeomanry had reached the line of the Sheria to Wa
Union, and the troops on the left were close to Hareira Redou
which was still occupied by the enemy.

Next day, the 7th, the situation remained practically u
changed on our extreme right, the enemy maintaining i
positions opposite our right flank-guard. In the Sheri
Hareira locality, the Hareira Tepe Redoubt was captur
at dawn. Tel el Sheria was captured at 4.0 a.m. and the li
was pushed forward about a mile to the north of Tel
Sheria. That night the enemy withdrew.

Meanwhile, on our extreme left, the bombardment of Ga:
had continued. Another attack was ordered to take pla
on the night of the 6th/7th. An attack was made at 11.
p.m. that night against Outpost Hill and Middlesex Hi
south of the town, which met with little opposition. " /
soon, after they had been taken, as patrols could be push
forward, the enemy was found to be gone. Early in th
morning, the main enemy force occupied the northern an
eastern defences of Gaza. Rearguards were still occupyin
Beit Hanun and the Atawinah and Tank System (part of th
Sihan group of works), from whence Turkish artillery co
tinued to fire on Gaza and Ali Muntar until dusk.

" As soon as it was seen that the Turks had evacuate
Gaza, on the morning of the 7th, a part of the force push
along the coast to the mouth of the Wadi Hesi, some 8 mil
north of Gaza, so as to turn the Wadi Hesi line and preve
the enemy making any stand there. This force reached th
Wadi Hesi by evening, and succeeded in establishing itse
on the north bank in the face of considerable opposition fro
a Turkish rearguard. Cavalry had already pushed on rour
the north of Gaza and become engaged at Beit Hanun with
enemy rearguard which maintained its position till night-fall
This brings our history down to the night of November 7th/8t

By the morning of the 8th the enemy were in retreat all along the line.

Meanwhile, what had been happening to our own party in the Apex ? The general plan of attack did not contemplate any advance from here. Nevertheless, it was necessary that this portion of the line should be firmly held, and it was more than likely that the enemy would try to create a diversion by raiding this inviting salient. By the end of October " liveliness " was increasing all round, and mutual bombardments were growing more intense. Fortunately, a large number of the shells fired by the enemy were " duds." We were puzzled at the time to know why duds figured so largely in this and following bombardments ; subsequent inspection of the enemy trenches afforded an explanation. Great lumps of ammunition had been formed by the enemy close to the guns, and these, for safety and concealment, had been placed in deep dug-outs. On the evening of the 27th October, a great thunderstorm burst over Gaza, causing the enemy considerable damage, flooding the dug-outs, and presumably damping the fuses and ruining their ammunition.

On the evening of the 3rd November, the enemy tried to create a diversion by raiding the Apex. On this evening we were sitting quietly having dinner in our headquarters dug-out, when sharp rifle fire was heard from the front line of the battalion on our right. We walked out, and saw a veritable Brock's Benefit display of Verey lights. A telephone message from our front line informed us that a considerable party of the enemy had crept quietly up, and were now prowling round our wire and trying to pick a way through. A hot fire from rifles, Lewis guns and machine guns, soon convinced the enemy of the uselessness of attempting, without artillery preparation, a raid against an alert enemy well entrenched with wire intact. They were beaten off, and withdrew to a fold in the ground a couple of hundred yards out in No Man's Land, where they were fired upon by our trench mortars. Nevertheless they managed to rally, and came forward again to the attack. This time their reception was no more encouraging than before; our artillery got into them with a barrage and they withdrew. Now they sent up a red Verey light signal, whereupon a hostile barrage came down upon our trenches, under cover of which they not only withdrew themselves, but also removed their killed and wounded. It is a part of their religion to spare no pains in removing their dead and giving them a decent burial. A couple of deserters crept into our lines towards the morning, from whom we were able to gather something about their side of the operations. Desertion was fairly common among the Turks about this time, partly because rations were poor, but mainly because they had no stomach for the fight that they knew to be imminent. In so far as this raid affected us, our trenches were badly smashed by the artillery, but our casualties were insignificant.

The next evening we sent a small patrol across No Man's Land, which, being boldly and pluckily led, crept right up to the enemy's trenches. Here they heard the sound of much traffic on the Gaza-Beersheba road, token doubtless of the impending withdrawal. More important from our immediate point of view, the patrol heard sounds of an enemy concentration in their front trenches, in apparent preparation for another raid on the Apex. Our artillery put salvoes at once upon those trenches; and the raid of that night proved a damp squib. About midnight we were wakened from our slumbers by a thunderstorm, the thunder, lightning and hail being provided by a deluge of bursting shells, splinters and shrapnel bullets. When the barrage lifted, glimpses were caught of the enemy moving along our front wire; but this raid never succeeded in forcing an entrance to our trenches.

We had every reason to "remember the fifth of November." It came in with a display of fireworks; it went out like an inferno. Profiting by his previous experience, the enemy shelled a portion of our front deliberately from early evening until dark, with the obvious intention of cutting the wire on a portion of our sector. At ten o'clock that night, down came another intensive bombardment, which lasted for an hour. Under cover of the darkness, the enemy even brought trench mortars on camels up to our wire to assist in the bombardment. Next morning the ground looked like a veritable sea beach after a wreck ; the litter consisted of splinters and duds of all sizes and descriptions, largely 5.9" H.Es. This hostile barrage made a really satisfactory job of the wire cutting. As soon as it lifted, the enemy's infantry made a determined effort to penetrate our line. During the bombardment our fellows had taken shelter in the narrow passage ways behind the traverses, and so lost no time, immediately the barrage lifted, in manning the fire-step. They at once got busy with rifles, Lewis guns and machine-guns, and gave the Turk, as he crossed the ruins of our wire, a distinctly warm reception. This proved more than enough for most of the enemy ; but a few brave spirits succeeded in entering our trench and throwing bombs. They were not supported by their fellows, and were soon disposed of. At length, up went the now familiar red light, down came the closing barrage, the enemy drew off and we were left in peace.

After these three abortive raids the Apex was left unmolested, except for occasional shelling on the 6th and 7th. On the 8th, we were relieved at the Apex by Lines of Communication troops, in order that we might take part in the pursuit of the enemy who were now in full retreat.

The quotations in this and the three following chapters, are from General Allenby's Despatch, dated the 16th December, 1917.

CHAPTER VIII

FULL CRY

WE have seen that during the night of the 7th/8th November, the enemy had retreated all along the line. The enemy opposite our right flank-guard withdrew toward Hebron, that is, north-east into the Judæan Hills. He was pursued for a short distance by the yeomanry, and some prisoners and camels were captured. The yeomanry were then recalled to rejoin the main body of the mounted troops for the more important work of the pursuit of the enemy main body. The enemy force that thus escaped into the hills there reorganized, and later descended to the Plain on the flank of our pursuing force with a view to creating a diversion; but of this, more anon.

On the afternoon of the 7th, when it was seen that our Sheria operations in the centre had been successful, the cavalry were ordered to push forward from there in the direction of Huj, which was the terminus of the enemy's branch railway line from Deir Sineid. Had this force of cavalry been able to push forward and join up with the cavalry that had worked round by the sea and were engaging the enemy rearguard at Beit Hanun, the bulk of the Turkish force engaged upon this front might have been surrounded and captured. The mounted troops on the right moved towards Huj, but met with considerable opposition from hostile rearguards. On this account, and through difficulty in watering horses, the consummation devoutly to be desired was not attained.

It will be remembered that the Gaza operations had the

ffect of almost turning the enemy's right flank as long ago
s November 2nd, and that, by the evening of the 7th, the
orce advancing along the coast had already established itself
n the north bank of the Wadi Hesi, some 6 miles or so behind
he enemy's defensive line.

Throughout the 7th, Turkish rearguards clung to Beit Hanun
nd to the Atawineh and Tank systems to the east of Ali
Iuntar. The effect of this was, that, when our troops eventu-
lly got under way in pursuit of the retreating Turks, those
ear the sea had several miles' start of those further inland.
his feature, a pursuit in echelon with the left flank advanced,
ontinued throughout these operations. And so we shall
ee that Jaffa fell into our hands some weeks before the cap-
ure of Jerusalem had even been attempted.

The bulk of the Turkish army retreated northwards along
he Coastal Plain. Here ran their railway, their main line of
ommunications, and also an excellent road from Gaza to
Jerusalem. Little or no opportunity was afforded of catch-
ng the disorganized enemy in narrow defiles, as happened
n the rout of the following autumn, but the open Plain offered
mple opportunities for a hasty retreat, of which the enemy
ully availed themselves.

"During the 8th, then, the advance was continued, and
nterest was chiefly centred in an attempt to cut off, if possible,
he Turkish rearguard which had held the Tank and Atawineh
ystems. Considerable captures of prisoners, guns, ammuni-
ion and other stores were made, especially at Huj and Deir
ineid, but no large formed body of the enemy was cut off.
he Turkish rearguards fought stubbornly and offered con-
iderable opposition." At this time the brunt of the work
vas being borne by the cavalry and the Royal Flying Corps,
he infantry not having yet been ordered forward. "Near
Iuj, a fine charge by some squadrons of the Worcester and
Warwick Yeomanry captured twelve guns, and broke the
esistance of a hostile rearguard."

"It soon became obvious from the reports of the Roy Flying Corps, who throughout the 7th and 8th attacked t retreating columns with bombs and machine-gun fire, a from other evidence, that the enemy was retiring in consid able disorganization, and could offer no very serious resistar if pressed with determination.

"Instructions were accordingly issued on the morning the 9th to the mounted troops, directing them on to the li El Tine-Beit Duras, that is, on to a line a little to the sout west of Junction Station, with orders to press the enen relentlessly. A portion of the infantry was ordered forwa in support.

"By the 9th, therefore, operations had reached the sta of a direct pursuit by as many troops as could be supplied far in front of the railhead."

The 54th Division had hitherto been principally engag between Gaza and the sea. The 52nd Division, therefor passed through the 54th and took up the pursuit along t coast, the pursuit along the Gaza—Jerusalem road falling the lot of the 75th.

On the night of the 8th, our regiment was relieved in t trenches at the Apex, and, on the 9th, the 75th Division co centrated behind the line, ready to take its part in the pu suit. Next day we all went forward in column of route. W crossed No Man's Land along the enemy's old front line trench by Ali Muntar. Having looked out upon this scene for mont through glasses, telescopes and periscopes, it was interestin now to obtain a close view of these fortress defences.

But there were other sights that met our eyes, sad and gru some, that can be better imagined than described. Portio of the enemy's wire, and of the gentle slopes in front, we littered with the remains of brave lads that had fallen in t sad days of March and April. It was strange that, in the own interests, the Turks had not buried these bodies. Instea they had left them lying there for months, beneath an almo tropical sun, and had actually fixed up their new wire entanglements over the unburied bodies. In some cases death had evidently been instantaneous. In others, where death had come more slowly, lads were to be found grasping open testaments or letters from home. It seemed so sad that these poor fellows, who had endured the hardships of the Desert and marched victoriously across Sinai, should, like Moses, have been privileged to see, but not to enter, the Promised Land.

After crossing No Man's Land, we marched along past pleasanter sights, great stacks of ammunition, gas cylinders, and other interesting captures. We enjoyed glimpses of how the enemy here had made himself comfortable ; still more did we enjoy glimpses of how we here had made the enemy uncomfortable. Huge craters there were, made by naval guns shelling from the sea. These guns had bombarded the enemy communications behind his front line, and had obtained direct hits on the track and rolling stock, causing a train or two, valuable booty, to fall into our possession. Bomb holes were to be seen, made by our aircraft in their efforts to destroy the bridges on the enemy's line of retreat.

We bivouacked on the night of the 10th at Deir Sineid. For the next two days we marched forward, close upon the heels of the pursuing cavalry, but not close enough yet to come into action or to deploy from column of route. All along our route lay evidences of the enemy's rout. At one time, we were passing a convoy of prisoners being shepherded along by a few cavalry ; at another, a party of refugees hurrying back with their worldly possessions to those homes to which they knew they could now return in safety. Here and there lay the body of some unfortunate Turk ; while all along the line lay the wreckage of vehicles and the carcases of transport animals.

Throughout these days the troops suffered considerably from thirst. A hot exhausting wind was blowing, and the men were heavily laden for long-distance route marching in a semi-tropical country. Water was the ever-recurring trouble. A little for the men to carry on with was generally procurable but the difficulty of watering the animals at times became acute. The usual tidings were, that there was plenty of water at the next village. When the next village was reached the tidings proved to be true, but so long was the queue of animals already waiting to be watered, that fresh arrivals stood but little chance. At many places the water was insufficient and " even when water was found in sufficient quantities, it was usually in wells and not on the surface ; consequently if the machinery for working the wells was damaged, or a sufficient supply of troughs was not available, the process of watering a large quantity of animals was slow and difficult."

Meanwhile, how were our cavalry progressing ? A glance at the map will show that, after the fall of Gaza, the next point of tactical importance in Palestine was Junction Station. With this in our hands, Jerusalem would be cut off from railway communication with the outer world, and quantities of rolling stock, supplies, war material and possibly prisoners should fall into our hands. While still pursuing the retreating enemy, therefore, the cavalry had been directed to make Junction Station their next objective.

The portion of the enemy's force that had withdrawn into the hills towards Hebron now made a descent from the hills to the Plain. Their object was to threaten the flank of our pursuing cavalry, create a diversion, and thus relieve the pressure from their main body. From Hebron, a couple of difficult tracks wind down the mountains to the village of Beit Jibrin, where they join a road coming from Bethlehem and Jerusalem. This latter road reaches the Plain and Beer-sheba railway at Arak el Menshiyeh. This was the spot then, towards which the counter-attack, or demonstration from the hills, was organized.

" It was obvious that the Hebron force, which was believed

be short of transport and ammunition, to have lost heavily, and to be in a generally disorganized state, could make no effective diversion, and that this threat could practically be disregarded. The Imperial Camel Corps, however, was ordered to move to the neighbourhood of Tel el Nejile, where it would be on the flank of any counterstroke from the hills; while orders were issued for the main pursuit to be pressed so that Junction Station might be reached with all speed. The Hebron group made an ineffective demonstration in the direction of Arak el Menshiyeh on the 10th, and then retired north-east so as to prolong the enemy's line towards Beit Jibrin."

Close to the sea, the advance-guard of the 52nd Division pushed on as far as Burkah on the 11th, and, on the 12th, the yeomanry pushed north and seized Tel el Murreh, on the right or northern bank of the Nahr Sukereir and close to its mouth.

"The operations of these days showed a stiffening of the enemy's resistance on the general line of the Wadi Sukereir, with centre about El Kustineh. Reports from the R.F.C. indicated the total hostile forces opposed to us on this line at about 15,000; and this increased resistance, coupled with the capture of prisoners from almost every unit of the Turkish force, tended to show that we were no longer opposed to rearguards, but that all the remainder of the Turkish Army, which could be induced to fight, was making a last effort to arrest our pursuit south of the important Junction Station. "On the morning of the 13th November, the situation was, that the enemy had strung out his force on a front of 20 miles from El Kubeibeh on the north to about Beit Jibrin to the south. The right half of his line ran roughly parallel to, and lay about five miles in front of, the railway to the north of Junction Station, which was the main line of supply from the north."

We have seen that our pursuit along the sea coast had a

considerable start of that further to the right, and the rapidi
of this pursuit had dictated to the enemy this rather unsat:
factory position which he was forced to take up. His rig
flank was already almost turned. In so far as he could o
so, he held a strong position on the line of heights runnin
north and south near the right flank of his position, on whic
heights stand the villages of Katrah and El Mughar.

The 12th was a day of preparation. On the 13th, an atta
was delivered against the enemy's position by the 75th Div
sion on the right and the 52nd on the left, the extreme rig
of the attack being protected by the Australian Mounte
Troops, who had pressed forward towards Balin Berkuss
and Tel es Safi. The country over which the attack too
place is open and rolling. It is dotted with small villag
surrounded by mud walls, with plantations of trees and thi
cactus hedges outside the walls. These hedges afford
admirable opportunities for the concealment of machine gun
In spite of heavy machine gun fire, the 75th attacked an
captured the village of El Mesmiye. A turning moveme
was directed against the enemy's right flank. There was
dashing charge of mounted troops, who galloped across tl
Plain under heavy fire and turned the enemy's position fro
the north. The Kahan El Mughar position, protecting tl
enemy's right flank, fell to the 52nd Division. After th
the enemy resistance weakened, and by the evening his forc
were in retreat. Early the following morning we occupi
Junction Station.

The enemy's flight from Junction Station was precipita
Two trains escaped shortly before our occupation, one of whi
was believed to have contained Von Kressenstein himse
Nevertheless our captures of rolling stock and material we
considerable. The enemy's army had now been broken in
two separate parts, which retired eastwards towards Jerusale
and northwards through Ramleh towards Tul Keram.

Throughout the 14th our mounted troops pressed on towa:

amleh and Ludd.   On the right, Naaneh, on the railway to
amleh, was attacked and captured in the morning.   On the
t, the New Zealand Mounted Rifles had a smart engage-
ent at Ayun Kara, 6 miles south of Jaffa, where the Turks
ade a determined counter-attack, and were only repulsed
the point of the bayonet.

On the morning of the 15th our mounted troops dislodged
hostile rearguard, which had taken up a position on the
gh ground, flanking the railway north of Junction Station,
d covering the main road from Jaffa to Jerusalem.   This
the site of Gezer, one of the most ancient of the Canaanitish
ies in Palestine, and one of the first objects of interest sought
the eye of the tourist on his journey up from Jaffa to Jeru-
lem.   Thus, commanding both the railway and the main
rusalem road, this position might have considerably delayed
r advance had it been held with determination.   As it was,
r mounted troops were able to occupy Ramleh and Ludd
at evening and to push forward patrols to within a short
stance of Jaffa.

Jaffa, the ancient port of Jerusalem, was occupied without
rther opposition on the evening of the 16th.

" The situation was now as follows.   The enemy's army,
t in two by our capture of Junction Station, had retired
rtly east into the mountains towards Jerusalem, and partly
rth along the Plain.   The nearest line on which these two
rtions could reunite was the line Tul Keram-Nablus."
lthough Jerusalem itself could still be supplied along the
ad connecting it with Nablus, or along the road across the
rdan to Ammam Station on the Hejaz Railway, yet " reports
om the R.F.C. indicated that it was the probable intention
the enemy to evacuate Jerusalem and withdraw to organize
the line Tul Keram-Nablus.

" On our side, the mounted troops had been marching and
ghting continuously since October 31st, and had advanced
distance of 75 miles measured in a straight line from Asluj

to Jaffa. The infantry, after their last fighting at Gaza, h advanced, in nine days, distances of from 40 to 70 miles, w two severe engagements and continual advanced-guard figl ing. The railway was being pushed forward as rapidly possible, and every opportunity was taken of landing sto at points along the coast ; but the landing of stores was dep dent on a continuance of favourable weather, and might any moment be stopped for several days together.

" A pause was therefore necessary to await the progress railway construction. But before our position in the Pl could be considered secure, it was essential to push forwa into the hills, and to obtain a hold of the one good road wh traverses the Judæan range from north to south, from Nab to Jerusalem."

CHAPTER IX

NEBY SAMWIL

OUR advance had hitherto been northwards along the low country, and had already reached a point on the Maritime Plain some miles north of the parallel of Jerusalem. It now wheeled to the right and struck into the Hills, with the object of getting astride the Jerusalem—Nablus road and of thus capturing the Holy City.

It will be remembered, from our survey of the geography of Palestine, that the ridge of the Judæan Hills runs approximately north and south, and that along the top of this ridge runs a first-class metalled road connecting Nablus with Jerusalem. From this ridge spurs run east and west down towards the Maritime Plain. These spurs are steep, bare and stony, and in places, precipitous, and are separated from one another by narrow valleys. Between such spurs, a few miles to the north-west of Jerusalem, sweeps down the Valley of Ajalon, with the villages of Beit-ur el-Foka (Beth-horon the Upper) and Beit-ur el-Tahta (Beth-horon the Lower), where Joshua won his memorable victory over the five kings of the Amorites. It was here that the routed hosts of the Amorites were pursued in panic, and near here that the sun and moon " stood still " at the bidding of Joshua. Further to the south, another gorge, or pass, roughly parallel to the Valley of Ajalon, leads down to the Plain, and along this pass runs the metalled road through Kurzet-el-Enab (Kirjath-Jearim), Saris and Bab-l-Wad, to Ramleh and Jaffa ; this is the road followed by the Pilgrims. Other paths were shown upon the map, but these were found to be mere tracks on the hillside or up the stony

F

beds of wadis, and, without considerable improvement, wer
impracticable for wheeled guns or transport. The only route
along which guns, other than mountain artillery, could I
moved, were the two first-class roads running northward
and westwards out of Jerusalem.

Ten miles north of Jerusalem, along the Nablus road, at
height of nearly 3,000 feet above sea level, is the village
Bireh. This commanding position overlooks the Jorda
Valley and all the surrounding country. This was the poin
which General Allenby decided to make his next objectiv
Reports had indicated that it was the probable intention
the enemy to evacuate Jerusalem, and in the known or su
pected state of the demoralisation of the enemy, it was fe
that considerable risks could be taken. Thus a bold an
immediate dash for Bireh seemed to be indicated. Furthe
more, an advance on this objective would take our forc
well clear of Jerusalem itself. And so this plan best conforme
with the determination that had previously been arrived a
that fighting should be within five miles of the Holy City.

The general idea of the operation was, that our troops shou
move up into the hills, some going by the Valley of Ajalo
and some by the main Jaffa—Jerusalem road as far as Ena
and thence by the "Roman road" running north-eas
Although it was thought likely that the Turks, reinforced fro
Damascus, and perhaps from Aleppo, would come down an
attack our new line, yet it was hoped that Bireh would I
reached before serious opposition was encountered. Th
enemy, however, changed his mind. Having, early in Novem
ber, decided to withdraw from Jerusalem, he now determine
to hold it till the bitter end. Turkish resistance stiffene
immensely. Pushed far into the hills, as were our advance
troops, and without much artillery support, it was foun
impossible for them to reach Bireh in the first stride; an
further operations upon a more elaborate scale had to I
undertaken before Jerusalem could be captured.

But we anticipate. Let us, then, return to the middle
of November, at which time our forces had captured, and were
holding, positions covering Jaffa, Ramleh and Junction Sta-
on. On the 17th November, the yeomanry commenced
to move from Ramleh through the hills direct on Bireh, via
he valley of Ajalon and Lower Beth-horon ; and, by the evening of the 18th, one portion of the yeomanry had reached
Lower Beth-horon, while another portion had occupied Shilta.

On the 19th, the infantry commenced its advance. Latron
and Anwas were captured in the morning. For nearly 4
miles, between Bab el Wad ($2\frac{1}{2}$ miles east of Latron) and Saris,
the Jaffa—Jerusalem road passes through a narrow gorge or
defile. The remainder of the day was spent in clearing this
defile up to Saris. " These narrow passes from the plain to
the plateau of the Judæan range have seldom been forced,
and have been fatal to many invading armies." The natural
facilities for defence in this pass were undoubtedly very
strong. " Had the attempt not been made at once, or had
it been pressed with less determination, the enemy would
have had time to reorganize his defences here, and the conquest
of the plateau would then have been slow, costly and precarious."

The character of the fighting now changed, and more nearly
resembled the mountain warfare of the north-west frontier
of India. The bulk of this hill fighting fell upon the 75th
Division, whose Indian experience proved invaluable. It
was interesting to note the points of resemblance and of dis-
tinction between hill fighting here and on the Indian frontier.

In India, frontier warfare is usually conducted against ill-
organized semi-savages, unarmed with artillery or machine
guns, but furnished with the instincts and cunning of beasts
of prey. Here the conditions were reversed. The enemy
were well provided with artillery and machine guns, both of
which they had had abundant opportunity to post advantage-
ously and use effectually ; whereas we had difficulties in get-

ting forward our guns and bringing them into action, and w
at times without artillery assistance. On the other ha
our troops surpassed the enemy in their familiarity w
mountain fighting.

Here, as in all mountain fighting, the cardinal princi
was piquetting the heights—that is to say, the necessity
sending up piquets from the advanced-guard, who deny to
enemy all commanding eminences, before the main body a
transport move up the defile which those eminences comma
Our piquets had frequently to fight their way up to the heigl
and to be prepared, on reaching the summit, to withstan
shelling or repulse a counter-attack. They had, therefo
to be stronger than is usually necessary in India, but had to
particularly careful not to concentrate too much upon
summit. In India, where the enemy generally fight a guer
warfare, hanging on to rearguards and cutting off straggle
the stiffest part of the fighting is to be expected during
subsequent withdrawal of the piquets from the heigl
Here, the fighting was done by the advanced-guard, and dur
the taking of the heights, subsequent withdrawal being ger
ally unmolested. Quickness in the attack was found to be
great value. In some cases the garrisons of heights w
surprised and captured before they could get away; m
than once the advanced-guard, pushing rapidly up the ro
were able to cut off such garrisons as they were coming do
the reverse slopes of their hills.

With regard to armament, our field artillery were abie
assist with their 4.2 inch howitzers, but the 18-pounder fi
guns, with their flat projectory, were, at this stage, found
be of little use. During later stages of this mountain warfa
the 18-pounder came again into its own; but that was w
suitable positions could be chosen deliberately, and wh
through the length of the range or the use of reduced char
they were able to drop their shells with a steep angle of desc
A high velocity gun, with a flat projectory, like our 18-poun

s two disadvantages in mountain warfare. When the gun
firing from behind a steep hill, the shell, on leaving the
n, is liable to strike the hill in front instead of clearing the
est. When the projectile reaches the distant ridge (behind
ich the enemy are presumably taking cover), the angle of
scent is not sufficiently steep to cause damage. More satis-
tory results were obtainable with howitzers, whose high
gle fire could both clear the forward crests and search the
verse slopes. Unfortunately, at this time, we had little
no mountain artillery up forward, while the wheeled guns
re often badly handicapped for want of good roads. We
d marched away from Gaza well enough supplied with
tillery for normal or plain country fighting, but scarcely
for this very different fighting in the mountains.

Another disadvantage under which we laboured, through
is abrupt merging from trench into mountain warfare, was
e overloading of the men. For the latter class of warfare
en must be lightly equipped ; in India, even the men's great-
ats are carried for them on pack-mules. Here, the men
re, of necessity, loaded up as for trench fighting, and were
rrying gas masks and extra bandoliers (50 rounds) of ammu-
tion, making a total of 170 rounds per man.

The key to success in modern mountain fighting proved
be the rapidity with which roads could be constructed for
inging forward artillery.

The defile up to Saris having been piquetted and cleared
the 19th, Enab was captured on the 20th in the face of
ganized opposition. Other infantry had moved from the
in along the more northern track (the Ajalon Valley route)
Berfilia and Beit Likia, and, on this same 20th, they cap-
red Beit Dukka. On the same day the yeomanry got to
thin 4 miles of the Nablus—Jerusalem road, but were stopped
strong opposition about Beithesnia, 3 or 4 miles west-south-
st of Bireh.

In this night it rained, as only in tropical and semi-tropical

countries it knows how. The men, clad in their Indian dri
were soaked immediately, and lay down on the road or in th
streets of Enab, or slept where they stood, the picture c
misery. An isolated Turk rushed down the road, determine
to sell his life dearly. But he could find nobody enthusiasti
enough to fight, or even to take sufficient interest in him t
accept his surrender ; until at last he found a military police
man, who, this being his job, had no alternative but to tak
him prisoner. At length dawn broke ; and it then becam
clear that Enab was under Turkish observation. So a col
night of rain was followed by a hot morn of fire.

From Enab, a "Roman road" leaves the main Jaffa—Jeru
salem road and strikes away north-east to Biddu, and thenc
towards Bireh. In Roman days, this may have been a
important road, but now it was found to be a mere rock
track, impassable for wheels, or for anything except infantr
and pack animals. On the morning of the 21st, a portio
of the 75th Division moved forward by this track, while anothe
portion of the Division was left at Enab to cover the flan
and demonstrate along the main Jerusalem road. Th
latter body drove hostile parties from Kushel, 2½ miles eas
of Enab, and secured this ridge. Meanwhile, progress along
the "Roman road" was slow. The track was under hostil
shell-fire, and it was found impossible to bring up guns t
support the advance of the infantry. The advanced guard
pushing on towards Bireh, had got as far as Biddu, when i
was held up there by intensive hostile shelling. The remain
der of the leading brigade thereupon captured a commanding
position about a couple of miles to the east of Biddu, and 2
miles short of the Jerusalem-Nablus road. This command
ing position was Neby Samwil.

Neby Samwil, one of the most prominent heights round
Jerusalem, must always have been a place of considerabl
importance. It is identified with Mizpeh, one of the citie
built by King Asa. Ecclesiastical tradition connects thi

place with Ramah, the birth and burial place of the prophet Samuel, whose tomb is said to lie under the Crusading Church, the ruins of which still exist here. To the honour of this prophet, the Moslems had erected a fine mosque upon this spot, which was a landmark for miles round. As subsequent events proved, Neby Samwil was the key to Jerusalem.

The question has been often asked : Who was the first to capture Neby Samwil ? The honour has sometimes been claimed for the 60th Division. No doubt that Division fought here, and fought well. But at least two other divisions, the 52nd and the 75th, had been fighting on this hill for a day or so before the arrival of the 60th. As a matter of fact, this hill, the " key " to Jerusalem, was first captured by a brigade of the 75th Division, in honour of which a " key " was there-after adopted as the proud distinguishing mark of this Division.

On Neby Samwil occurred some of the bitterest fighting in the Palestine campaign. Both sides realized the vital importance of the position. All the first night the hill was distinctly unhealthy. The trees were infested with snipers who picked off our men in the bright moonlight. Some refuge from the sniping was procurable inside the Mosque, but the Turkish artillery had no compunction in shelling the build-ing and bringing it down in ruins. As the night progressed, more troops were poured on to the hill. The snipers were hunted down and summarily dealt with. Machine guns were established in the ruined Mosque and other appropriate posi-tions, and preparations made to hold the hill at all costs. Towards the morning the Turks delivered a determined counter-attack. During the 22nd, the enemy made two counter-attacks on the Neby Samwil Ridge, which we repulsed. In one case, the Ghurkhas, having run out of ammunition, hurled down rocks and boulders upon the heads of the ascend-ing enemy. At one time the Mosque was deserted by all except one machine-gun officer, who continued to work his gun single-handed. By this time the 52nd Division had come up and were, in some cases relieving, in some fighting side by side with, the 75th.

On the 23rd and on the 24th, determined and gallant attacks were made on the strong positions to the west of the Nablus road held by the enemy, who had brought up reinforcements and numerous machine guns, and could support his infantry by artillery fire from guns placed in position along the main road. Our artillery, from lack of roads, could not be brought up to give adequate support to our infantry, and both attacks failed. The yeomanry, who by the afternoon of the 21st had got to within a couple of miles of the Nablus road, were heavily counter-attacked, and fell back, after bitter fighting, on Beit-ur el-Foka (Upper Beth-horon).

This fighting had been taking place over classical and sacred ground. Troops fighting on Neby Samwil looked down upon the Holy City, still in the hands of the Turk. Our advanced dressing station was established in the beautiful monastery on the traditional site of Emmaus ; here the men were dying on the very spot that the risen Christ had been made known to His disciples in the breaking of bread.

" The positions reached on the evening of the 21st practically marked the limit of the progress in this first attempt to gain the Nablus road. Positions had been won from which our final attack could be prepared and delivered with good prospects of success. Nevertheless, it was evident that a period of preparation and organization would be necessary before an attack could be delivered in sufficient strength to drive the enemy from his positions"

Orders were accordingly issued to consolidate the position gained and prepare for relief. The 60th Division had been lent to the 21st Corps, and had already taken their place in the fighting on Neby Samwil. Now the 21st Corps were gradually relieved and moved over to the left ; while the operations about Jerusalem were taken over by the 20th Corps.

TO NABLUS

BEITIN

BIREH

MUKAMAS

TO R JORDAN
EL SALT &
AMMAN
JERICHO

BI SAMWIL

BIT IKSA

JERUSALEM
MOUNT OF OLIVES

JORDAN VALLEY

BEIT SURAFAT

SKETCH MAP
OF
COUNTRY ROUND JERUSALEM
ILLUSTRATING THE OPERATIONS FOR
THE CAPTURE OF THE CITY

BETHLEHEM

MILES 0   1   2   3   4   5   10

DEAD
SEA

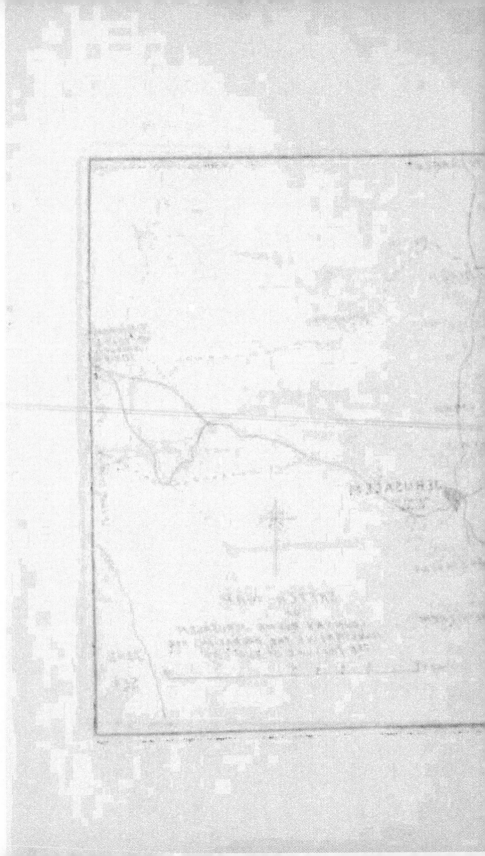

CHAPTER X

JERUSALEM

LET us trace the fortunes of the 20th Corps, whom we last saw engaged in the fighting about Beersheba. After the fall of Gaza and Beersheba, most of the mounted troops went forward in pursuit of the enemy along the Maritime Plain. These were closely followed up and supported by the 21st Corps, i.e. the 52nd and 75th Divisions, with the 54th following close upon their heels. It was impossible at this time to supply more than a limited number of troops far forward of railhead. So the Divisions of the 20th Corps after their successful operations at Beersheba and Sheria, were first moved backwards to rest and re-equip, before going forward again into the field zone. Of these 20th Corps Divisions, the 60th were the first to go forward. Following along the main Gaza—Junction Station road, in the footsteps of the 75th and 54th Divisions, the 60th arrived at Junction Station on the 22nd November, on which date the head-quarters of the 20th Corps also moved up to, and opened at, Junction Station. The 60th Division were now lent to the 21st Corps. They moved forward next day, following along the Jerusalem road to Enab, and about the 24th or 25th began to take their place in the fighting on the Neby Samwil ridge. Shortly after the 60th came forward the 74th. By the time that they got sufficiently far forward, the 20th Corps were taking over from, and relieving, the 21st, and the 74th Division soon found itself in the zone of operations to the west and north-west of Jerusalem. The 10th Division remained in the neighbourhood of Gaza for a few weeks, until the possibilities of supply permitted their also going forward. The 53rd Division did not go forward by the Maritime Plain at all. They remained about Beersheba until the 4th December. Then they moved forward, without meeting with opposition, along the higher road, that is, through Hebron towards Bethlehem; and subsequently arrived in the hills at such time and place as their presence was required for manœuvring the enemy out of Jerusalem.

While these reliefs were in progress, several determined counter-attacks were delivered by the enemy in their attempt to dislodge us from the positions of advantage that we had already gained. At this time our line was, of necessity, somewhat thinly held, especially towards the sea. The Imperial Camel Corps, whom we last saw protecting the right flank of the pursuit from the threat near Beit Jibrin, had been moved across to the extreme left, where they and cavalry held positions on the north bank of the River Auja, protecting Jaffa. Further to the right, the line was carried on by the 54th Division, who thus linked up, along the ridge north of the Valley of Ajalon, with the 52nd and 75th Divisions then fighting in the neighbourhood of Neby Samwil. " On the 25th November our advanced posts north of the River Auja were driven back across the river. An attack on the night of the 29th succeeded in penetrating our outpost line north-east of Jaffa; but next morning the whole hostile detachment, numbering 150, was surrounded and captured by the Australian Light Horse. Attacks were also delivered against the left flank of our position in the hills from Beit-ur el-Foka to El Burj and the Neby Samwil ridge. One such attack was delivered on the 30th near El Burj, when a counter-attack by Australian Light Horse took 200 prisoners and practically destroyed the attacking battalion. There was particularly heavy fighting between El Burj and Beit-ur el-

Foka, but all these attacks were successfully resisted and severe losses were inflicted on the enemy. All efforts by the enemy to drive us off the Neby Samwil ridge were completely repulsed.

"These attacks in no way affected our positions nor impeded the progress of our preparations. Favoured by a continuance of fine weather, preparations for a fresh advance against the Turkish positions west and south of Jerusalem proceeded rapidly. Existing roads and tracks were improved and new ones constructed to enable heavy and field artillery to be placed in position and ammunition and supplies brought up. The water supply was also developed. By December 4th all reliefs were complete." A line was then held from Kushel, about 5 miles to the west of Jerusalem, along the ridge that runs north-east some 3 or 4 miles to Neby Samwil. From this point, the line bent back at a right angle, and ran along the northern ridge of the Valley of Ajalon through Beit Izza and Beit Dukka to Beit-ur el-Tahta (Beth-horon the Lower), from which point it was carried west and north-west to the sea.

The enemy held a line approximately facing our Kushel-Neby Samwil line, protecting Jerusalem from attack from the west or north-west, his front line being distant about three miles from the city, and artillery and machine guns being posted in the outskirts of the city itself. He had two good lines of supply or retreat, namely the north road from Nablus and the eastern road through Jericho and across the Jordan to Amman Station on the Hejaz Railway. It will be remembered that, in the words of the Psalmist, "The Hills stand round about Jerusalem." The Turks were able to select positions of considerable natural strength in these surrounding hills. In fact, the country is one continual succession of hills and valleys, the hillsides steep and rocky, the valleys deep and strewn with boulders. These positions of natural strength the enemy had improved by the construction of trenches and strong points and other devices of modern field engineering.

The general idea of the operations for the capture of Jerusalem was the simultaneous pressure of three Divisions, whereby the enemy should be driven off his main roads, and the city be isolated, and so forced to surrender. The 60th and 74th Divisions had already arrived in the fighting zone and were occupying positions in the line, the 60th on the right, about Kushel, and the 74th about Neby Samwil. On December 4th the 53rd Division commenced their march from Beersheba up the Hebron—Jerusalem Road. No opposition was met and, by the evening of the 6th, the head of this column was ten miles north of Hebron. The infantry were directed to reach the Bethlehem area by the 7th, and a line about three miles south of Jerusalem by dawn on the 8th. The 8th was the date fixed for the commencement of the renewed operations against Jerusalem.

" On the 7th the weather broke, and for three days rain was almost continuous. The hills were covered with mist at frequent intervals throughout the fighting, rendering observation from the air and visual signalling impossible." Great was the discomfort caused to the men by this rain, fog and mud. The cold was intense, and soldiers who had borne the brunt of a long day's fighting could not sleep, but just lay huddled together longing for the dawn. An even more serious effect of the rain was to jeopardise the supply arrangements by converting the roads into seas of liquid mud, rendering them almost impassable, in places quite impassable for camel and mechanical transport.

By dawn on the 8th, all the troops were in their allotted positions, except the 53rd Division. It had been recognized that these troops on the extreme right might be delayed and fail to reach the positions assigned to them by dawn on the 8th, and arrangements had accordingly been made for the protection of our right flank west of Jerusalem in case of such delay occurring. This contingency did occur. The 53rd Division was held up by mud and fog, and by roads blown up by the enemy, so that, by the morning of the 8th, it was still some distance south of Jerusalem ; on that day it exercised little or no influence on the fighting.

During the darkness of the night of the 7th/8th December, and in weather such as we have described, portions of the 60th Division clambered down the mountain side, crossed the deep wadi bed in front of the right of our line, and crept up the steep terraced sides of the opposite ridge where ran a portion of the Turkish line. One brigade was to make a frontal attack, while another was to turn the left flank of the enemy's position, by scaling a spur to the south-west of the village of Ain Karim. These two brigades stormed the main line of works before daylight and captured the western defences of Jerusalem. Considerable rifle and artillery fire was experienced from the outskirts of Jerusalem, so that it was necessary for our troops to throw back their right and form a defensive flank facing eastwards towards the city. Artillery support from our own guns soon became difficult, owing to the length of the advance and the difficulty of moving guns forward. It thus became difficult for these troops to attain their subsequent objectives in the direction of the Nablus road north of Jerusalem. Accordingly, it was decided, early in the afternoon, to consolidate the line gained and resume the advance next day, when the right column (the 53rd Division) would be in a position to exert its pressure.

Meanwhile, the task of the 74th Division was to swing forward, with their left resting and pivoting on Neby Samwil, to capture Beit Iksa village and works, and so to swing forward to the Nablus road. They each captured their first objective, and we were preparing for a further advance. But the delay on the right made it desirable to check for the time the advance on the left, and to consolidate the positions already attained.

By nightfall, our line ran from Neby Samwil to the east
Beit Iksa, through Lifta, to a point of about $1\frac{1}{2}$ miles we
of Jerusalem, whence it was thrown back facing east. Thu
our main line had swung forward, circling on its pivot at Ne
Samwil, with its extreme right flank refused. The refuse
right flank afforded protection against the fire coming fro
the city. The main directions of our advance, howeve
now menaced, not so much Jerusalem itself, as the main Nabl
road a few miles to the north of the city. All the enemy
prepared defences west and north-west of Jerusalem ha
been captured, and our troops were within a short distan
of the Nablus—Jerusalem Road.

That night the Turks withdrew. On the following mor
ing, the 9th December, the 74th and 60th Divisions, drivin
back rearguards, occupied a line across the Nablus—Jerusale
road 4 miles north of Jerusalem.

In the meantime, the 53rd Division had arrived on th
scene of operations to the south of Jerusalem. They bo
right-handed, cleared the Mount of Olives, which comman
Jerusalem from the east, drove the enemy away eastward
and occupied a position east of Jerusalem across the Jerich
road.

These operations isolated Jerusalem. At about noon o
the 9th December, 1918, the city was surrendered.

Two days later General Allenby made his official ent
into Jerusalem. It was a simple ceremony. The Genei
entered the city on foot, preceded by his aides-de-camp, ar
accompanied by the commanders of the French and Itali
detachments, by the French, Italian and American milita
attachés, and by a few members of the General Staff. Ou
side the Jaffa Gate he was received by the Military Governe
and a guard of honour composed of representatives of troo
from the various portions of the British Empire, which h
taken part in the recent operations ; while, inside the wal
were small parties from the French and Italian detachmer

which those countries had sent to assist us in Palestine. Inside the city, at the base of the Tower of David, the ceremony was concluded by the reading of the Proclamation. Its terms promised that every person could pursue his lawful business without interruption, and that every sacred building, monument, holy spot, shrine, traditional site, endowment, pious bequest, or customary place of prayer of whatsoever form of the great religions of mankind, would be maintained and protected according to the existing customs and beliefs of those to whose faiths they were sacred.

CHAPTER XI

THE HOLY CITY[1]

IT is beyond the scope of this book to attempt a detaile
history of Jerusalem. It cannot, however, fail to interes
those readers who have followed us thus far, if we glance at
few incidents in the history of this sacred spot.

Of little importance, perhaps non-existent, in the days o
the Patriarchs, and still in the hands of the Jebusites throug
the days of Joshua, the Judges, and Samuel, it first spran
into fame about a thousand years before Christ when it wa
captured by King David, who made it his capital. Solomo
built his temple on Mount Moriah, and prayed to Jehova
that He would especially hear the prayers of His people whe
they prayed toward the city which He had chosen and th
House which Solomon had built for His name. Then di
this city become, and has ever since remained, the sacre
city of the Jews.

With the advent of Christ, born within a few miles of it
walls, Who here preached and healed, instituted His Hol
Sacrament, suffered under Pontius Pilate, was crucified, dea
and buried and the third day rose again from the dead, Wh
here laid the foundations of the most beautiful religion tha
the world has ever seen, Jerusalem became and has ever sinc
remained, the sacred city of the Christian.

[1] Much of the material in this Chapter is derived from Milman
History of the Jews, W. Besant and E. H. Palmer's *Jerusalem*, ar
George Adam Smith's *Historical Geography of the Holy Land*,
which my acknowledgments are accordingly due.

And then, six hundred years later, came the rise of Islam. The great prophet Mahomet, in evolving his religion, based his teaching upon the principles of Judaism and Christianity, the prophets of which were to be honoured, including "the prophet David" and "the Prophet Christ." So, in accordance with the prayer of Solomon, and until the antagonism between Judaism and Islam led to the substitution of Mecca, it was towards Jerusalem that devout Moslems were required to turn when they prayed. From Mount Moriah did Mahomet, as his followers believe, miraculously ascend to heaven. And so did Jerusalem become, and has ever since remained, no less a sacred city of the Mahomedan.

Thus it will be seen that Jerusalem, the sacred city of three mighty religions, became the most holy city in the world, the poetical prototype of heaven.

Jerusalem, situate away on the hills and far from the main trading and military route, was of but little commercial or strategical importance. Yet we readily understand how its religious value caused it so often to become the goal and prize of contending creeds and armies. Sometimes the motive was religious antagonism, as with Antiochus Epiphanes and Titus ; sometimes it was religious devotion, as with the Maccabees and Crusaders. Pitiful though it be, yet, throughout the ages, the City of the Prince of Peace has been associated with the most terrible scenes, the most savage excesses, in the whole dreadful drama of war.

Not once nor twice in the reigns of the Kings of Judah and Israel, did Jerusalem resound with the clash of arms. Although, after the fall of the northern kingdom, it was delivered by divine intervention from the invasion of Sennacherib, yet its submersion by the rising tide of Babylon could not long be averted. The evil day had only been postponed and, in 607 B.C., Jerusalem fell before Nebuchadnezzar, before that power which, like Turkey of yesterday, dominated the whole stretch of country from the Persian Gulf to the border of Egypt. Twenty years later, Jerusalem, with the Temple of Solomon, was destroyed, the city, palaces and temple being levelled in one, and the population were put to death or led away captive to Babylon.

When, some years later, the capital of the Babylonian was captured by the Persians and their empire annexed, the Jews were permitted to return to Jerusalem. In the sixth and fifth centuries B.C. the temple and walls were rebuilt under Ezra and Nehemiah, and Jerusalem took a fresh lease of life as a Jewish city.

In the fourth century B.C., when Alexander the Great marched southwards through Syria to Egypt, securing the Mediterranean littoral before embarking on his expedition into Asia, overthrowing Tyre in his march and totally destroying Gaza, the Jews no doubt made their submission, and their city thus escaped destruction.

After the death of Alexander, Judæa did not escape the anarchy which ensued during the internecine warfare waged by his generals and successors. In 321 B.C., Ptolemy I, King of Egypt, advanced against Jerusalem, and, assaulting it on the Sabbath, the Jew's day of rest, met with no resistance. He is said to have carried away 100,000 captives, whom he settled in Alexandria and Cyrene. The founding of a Syro-Grecian kingdom in Northern Syria brought Judæa again into the unfortunate situation of a buffer state. Jerusalem seemed doomed to be among the prizes of an interminable warfare between the Ptolemies of Egypt and the Seleucidæ of Syria and in turns vassal to each.

At the commencement of the second century B.C. Judæa passed into the hands of the Syrian King Antiochus the Great who at once proceeded to ingratiate himself with the whole nation. It was not the tyranny of foreign sovereigns, but the unprincipled ambition of their own native rulers, that led to calamities little less dreadful than the Babylonian captivity. Jason, the High Priest, had been dispossessed by his brother

enelaus, by double dealing with the Syrian King, who at
his time was Antiochus Epiphanes. A rumour of the King's
eath having reached Palestine in 170 B.C., Jason seized the
pportunity and revolted against his brother Menelaus. But
he rumour was false.

"The intelligence of the insurrection, magnified into a
eliberate revolt of the whole nation, reached Antiochus.
e marched without delay against Jerusalem, put to death
three days' time 40,000 of the inhabitants, and seized as
any more to be sold as slaves. He entered every court
the Temple, pillaged the treasury, and seized all the sacred
ensils. He then commanded a great sow to be sacrificed
the altar of burnt offerings, part of the flesh to be boiled,
d the liquor from the unclean animal to be sprinkled over
ery part of the Temple ; and thus desecrated with the most
ious defilement the sacred place which the Jews had con-
dered for centuries the one holy spot in all the Universe." [1]

Two years afterwards, Antiochus determined to exterminate
e Hebrew race from the face of the earth. This produced
e revolt of the Jews under Mattathias, whose illustrious
n, Judas Maccabæus, founded the Maccabæan dynasty.
y 128 B.C., the Jews, under John Hyrcanus, recovered their
mplete independence, which they maintained until compelled
acknowledge the dominion of Rome.

But the native rulers could not govern for long without
ssension. Soon were two more competitors, Aristobulus
d Hyrcanus, quarrelling about the succession to the Jewish
rone. The republic of Rome, having trampled under foot
e pride and strength of the great Asiatic monarchies, assumed
right of interfering in the affairs of every independent king-
m. The ambassadors of Aristobulus and Hyrcanus appeared
fore Pompey, who was then in Syria and was at the zenith
his power. After subjugating Arabia, Pompey, in 63 B.C.,
arched directly into Judæa. Espousing the candidature

[1] Milman.

of Hyrcanus, Pompey marched against Jerusalem, within t
walls of which he was admitted by the party of Hyrcan
Aristobulus and his supporters, with the priesthood, withdr
to the Temple and prepared for an obstinate defence.
the end of three months, and after great loss of life, the Roma
made themselves masters of the Temple. " The conduct
the Roman General excited at once the horror and the admir
tion of the Jews. He entered the Temple, and even pen
trated and profaned with his heathen presence the Holy
Holies. All the riches he left untouched, and the Temple
commanded to be purified from the carnage of his soldiers.
He stipulated the tribute which the country was to pa
demolished the walls of the city, and nominated Hyrcan
to the priesthood, though without the royal diadem. T
magnanimity of Pompey, in respecting the Treasures of t
Temple, could not obliterate the deeper impression of jew
hatred excited by his profanation of the sacred precincts.

From this time forward Judæa becomes more and mc
under the shadow of Rome. The walls of Jerusalem w
rebuilt by Antipater, and later, the Temple, which had beco
much dilapidated, was demolished, and rebuilt in great magn
cence by Herod the Great. He was the last King of Jud
with any semblance of autonomy, and, in the year A.D.
Palestine was annexed to the Roman Empire.

We pass over the incidents in the Life and death of our Lo
which, at the time, could have but little affected curr
events, but which were destined to influence so deeply t
subsequent history, not merely of Palestine but of the wh
world. And we come to the cataclysm of which Our L
had been the sorrowful yet unerring Prophet.

Blinded by religious fanaticism, and convinced that G
must fight upon their side and give victory to His cho
people, be their conduct never so cruel and their bearing ne
so arrogant, the Jewish race, though a mere handful of m

[1] Milman.

offered war to the mistress of the world. With little military organization or training, divided by factions and torn asunder by internal dissensions, they yet dared to defy the mighty power of Rome. They defeated the ill-starred expedition of Cestius Gallus, and inflicted upon the Roman arms the most terrible disgrace they had ever endured in the East. But the triumph was short-lived; a terrible revenge was at hand. It was in this year, A.D. 70, that Titus laid siege to the city. At the time, its population was swollen ten or twenty-fold by the pilgrims attending the Passover. The reserves of food were destroyed in faction fights even before the Romans arrived outside the city walls. " Of all wretched and bloody sieges in the world's history, few, if any, have been more wretched or more bloody than the siege of Jerusalem by Titus. Fierce and bloody as was the fighting, the deaths from sickness and famine were yet more terrible. Dead bodies were thrown out into the valleys, where they lay rotting, a loathsome mass. The number of those who died in the siege were estimated at 600,000. At night, miserable, starving wretches would steal into the ravines to gather roots for food; here they were pounced upon by ambushed Romans and crucified by hundreds next morning in full view of the battlements." [1] Gradually the assaulting Romans got possession of portions of the city, yet the portions still uncaptured refused to surrender, their defenders still hoping against hope for a divine intervention, as in the days of Sennacherib. At length the city fell. The Romans, pouring in, began by slaying indiscriminately. Tiring of butchery, they turned their thoughts to plunder, but stood aghast at the houses filled with dead and putrefying corpses. The Temple of Herod was burnt, the city was desolate, while those whose miseries had not been relieved by death, were carried away into yet more miserable slavery or to a death more ignominious at Rome. As a Jewish city, Jerusalem had perished for ever.

[1] Milman.

Sixty years later, Jerusalem was rebuilt by the Emperor Hadrian. He resolved to suppress altogether the troublesome and turbulent Judaism. The measures which he took caused the Jews to rise against him under Barcochebas. This was the wildest and the most bloodthirsty of all the Jewish revolts but it was the last. Jerusalem having been recaptured Hadrian converted it into a Roman colony, forbade Jews to approach, and built a temple of Jupiter on the site of the Temple.

It was when the Roman Emperor Constantine embraced Christianity, and his mother Helena discovered the true Cross and the Holy Places, that Jerusalem came again into prominence. Thereafter, churches and monasteries sprung up throughout Palestine, which thus, for a time, became thoroughly Christianized, under the Christian Emperors of Rome and Byzantium. But the seventh century saw the fall of the Christian ascendancy in Syria. In A.D. 614, the Persians, under Chosroes, swept through the land, massacring the Christians wholesale, and destroying most of their churches, including the Church of the Holy Sepulchre. The withdrawal of the Persians was followed by a brief return of Christian ascendancy lasting but eight years, under the Emperor Heraclius. And then, in 637, Jerusalem fell to the growing power of Islam. It was this new religion, with a calendar only dating from A.D. 622, which was to control the future destinies of the Holy City.

Islam arose at Mecca and Medina in barren and uninviting Arabia. When it started on that expansion, whereby it overspread half of the known world, Syria, from its situation, was naturally the first country to tempt its restless and devoted Arab warriors. Within ten years of the Hegira, or commencement of the Mahomedan era, we find the followers of the Prophet already in Syria. The Byzantine army was overwhelmed at the battle of the Yarmuk, and the Arabs laid siege to Jerusalem. The city capitulated to Omar, who granted terms of comparative magnanimity. His terms gave to the Christians security of person and property, safety of their churches, and non-interference on the part of Mahomedans with their religious exercises, houses or institutions. Upon the site of the Temple, which had been systematically defiled by the Christians out of abhorrence for the Jews, but which was honoured by the Moslems as the spot from which Mahomed ascended to heaven, was now erected the Mosque of Omar. This site became to the Mussulman, the most venerated spot in Jerusalem, as was the Church of the Holy Sepulchre to the Christian. When, in after years, pilgrimages to Mecca were temporarily interrupted, devout Mahomedans made the pilgrimage to Jerusalem instead.

For the next few centuries Christian and Muslim lived together upon a fairly workable basis of toleration. Massacres of Christians and destruction of their churches occurred periodically, either in revenge for Christian successes elsewhere, or in connexion with other Mussulman disorders when mutual assassination was popular. But, on the whole, pilgrims, who at this time swarmed from all over Europe to visit the Holy Places at Jerusalem, were allowed to do so comparatively unmolested—that is, they were probably not robbed more in Palestine than in other professedly Christian countries through which they had to pass along their road. Had the Arab Mussulman remained master of Jerusalem, the Christians of Europe would probably have remained content with the situation.

A change came in the year 1077. Jerusalem was then taken by the Turks, who had conquered all Asia Minor and were already threatening the Byzantine Empire in Europe. The treatment which the Christian pilgrims now received at Jerusalem aroused intense indignation in Europe, chiefly stimulated by the preaching of Peter the Hermit. Other motives there were, such as the protection of the Byzantine Empire from the menaces of the Turk, the desire of the Latin Church to prevail

over the Byzantine, and the temptations always offered :
a holy war of loot upon earth and salvation in heaven. Neve
theless, there undoubtedly spread, throughout Western Europ
a mighty wave of religious enthusiasm which was sincere.

The first Crusade was mainly recruited in France. Gre
were the vicissitudes through which the Crusaders passed c
their pilgrimage through Europe and Asia Minor, large
through quarrels with their fellow-Christians before the Turl
had even been encountered or their country entered. Havir
defeated the Turks at Antioch, the army marched south alor
the coast and at length reached and besieged Jerusalem. C
the numbers that set out from Western Europe, probab
not less than a million, only a remnant of twenty thousar
fighting men, with an equal number of followers, had reache
the Holy City. Though thus decimated and war wear
the Crusaders were ecstatic with religious fervour ; St. Georg
was said to have appeared to them clad in shining armou
the Saracens gave way, and Jerusalem was taken by assau
The usual massacre of the inhabitants followed, and estimal
of the slain vary from forty to a hundred thousand. In 10
was established the Christian kingdom of Jerusalem, the kin
dom of the Crusaders. Latin in creed, French in nationalit
feudal in character and precarious in existence. The sta
of affairs seems now rather to have resembled the relationsh
which formerly existed between the Hebrews and the Phili
tines, or, even more analogously, that between the Itali
city-states of the Middle Ages. Most of the cities of Palesti
were gradually annexed by the Christians, but some, notab
Askalon, did not pass out of the hands of the Saracens f
many decades. Accordingly, wars became matters of almo
annual occurrence, and " never, during the whole eighty yea
of its existence, was the kingdom of Jerusalem free from w
and war's alarms." [1] The bulk of the original Crusade
left alive soon returned to their homes in Europe. The

[1] Besant & Palmer.

as little or no native Christian population on which to draw,
and the kingdom became dependent for the support of its
army, both as to men and money, on the pilgrims that swarmed
from Europe to Jerusalem; naval assistance was given by
Genoese and by Venetians, more, alas, from motives of com-
merce than of piety. Religious enthusiasm had been capable
of conquering and establishing this kingdom, but it proved
quite unequal to the tasks of sustenance or protection. And
so, after eighty years of romance and trouble, of love and
war, of lust and murder, often inflicted, more often endured,
this kingdom fell, because it had no sure foundation.

The decline and fall of the Latin kingdom of Jerusalem forms
a sordid story of jealousy, and intrigue, of futile ambition and
divided counsels, of perjury and perfidy. The Crusaders
intermarried with the women of the country, and, except so
far as it was constantly recruited from Europe, the race rapidly
degencrated. With no resources at their back, except the
charity of Europe, the Crusaders yet had dreams of worldly
aggrandisement, which included in their ken the whole of
Egypt and Syria. The Second Crusade of 1146-9 came, not
to conquer, but to support and defend this already tottering
kingdom. It did that kingdom more harm than good, for
it drained Europe of its potential pilgrims, anticipating and
exhausting the natural flow of men and money on which the
kingdom had come to rely, and dissipated them on a futile
attempt to annex Damascus.

The Knights Templars, the feudal barons of the country,
built castles throughout the land, and lived at constant vari-
ance with the King and central government. Every baron
fought for his own land and for his own aggrandisement.
The kingdom of Jerusalem was fast tottering to its fall.

It was in 1187 that Saladin, having made himself master of
Egypt and of Damascus, attacked Tiberias, as a first step
towards overthrowing the kingdom of Jerusalem. The
Crusaders moved against him from Seffuriyeh. It was July,

and the Crusaders were absolutely without water ; the Sa
cens, with Lake Tiberias at their back, had abundance. T
Crusaders, suffering terribly from thirst, nevertheless attack
The result of the battle was a foregone conclusion. Here,
the Horns of Hattin, the Mount of Beatitudes, was the C
saders' army destroyed and the power of the Christian cc
pletely crushed. Jerusalem itself, after a short, fierce strug
fell in the following October. The inhabitants were
put to the sword. Huge ransoms were paid and the Christi
population allowed to disperse throughout Syria. Jerusal
had passed again (it seemed as if for ever) into the hands
the Mahomedan.

"The news of the fall of Jerusalem was received in Eurc
with a thrill of horror and indignation."[1] Thereupon
forth the Third Crusade, that which is identified with Richa
I of England. Travelling by sea, these Crusaders avoided
horrible sufferings inevitable to the crossing of Asia Min
Acre was captured in 1190, by the Crusaders, after a si
lasting for two years. Thence they marched southwar
through Cæsarea to Jaffa, fighting on their way the great bat
of Assur, when Saladin was defeated. But Richard, inste
of marching upon Jerusalem, which lay in his grasp, vacilla
and negotiated. At length he decided to go up against Je
salem. Some twenty miles from the city he stopped. Aga
he vacillated. Dissensions broke out between the Duke
Burgundy and King Richard. The design of besieging Je
salem was given up, and the army slowly and sadly return
to Jaffa. Thereupon, in 1192, a peace was concluded, where
the sea coast, from Jaffa to Acre, was ceded to the Fran
but Jerusalem still remained in the hands of the Sarace

There were several more Crusades. None of them (unl
we except the treaty of the excommunicated Frederick
1229) ever reached Jerusalem. Some of them never ev
reached Palestine, being shamefully diverted to other purpos

[1] Besant & Palmer.

Saddest of all was the Children's Crusade, when fifty thousand poor misguided children followed the Cross (like the Pied Piper of Hamelin) to slavery, dishonour, or death. But these form no part of the history of Jerusalem.

In 1244, we find Christian and Saracen making common cause in Palestine against the Kharezmians. These Mongols, who only appeared on the stage of history for a brief period of four years, swept through the country, captured Jerusalem, massacred all on whom they could lay hands, Moslem and Christian alike, and destroyed such sacred relics as they could find. Then, defeated by the Egyptians, they perished out of history as suddenly as they had appeared.

In 1291, the Christians, by this time reduced to their last stronghold of Acre, were finally expelled by the Moslems from Palestine—and that was the end of the Crusades. Europe became reconciled to the fact that the Kingdom of Christ is a Kingdom, not of the sword but of the soul. And so, the watchword by which the Crusades were inspired now became the consolation of their end—" Dieu le veut."

In 1400, Syria and Palestine fell under another Mongol invasion by Timoor the Tartar (Tamerlane). In 1517, Palestine was annexed to the Ottoman Empire under Selim I, of which Empire it has since formed an integral part. At the close of the eighteenth century, Napolean marched through the country, defeating the Turks at Gaza and on the Plain of Esdraelon, but was forced to withdraw. In 1832, Mohammad Ali, having thrown off the Turkish yoke in Egypt, conquered Syria, but nine years later, through the action of the European Powers, the country was restored again to the Ottoman Porte.

In so far as any principles can be deduced from this history, they seem to show that Jerusalem, situated as it is, could never become the capital of a great Empire. On the other hand, this city, coveted by so many races and creeds, must be safeguarded by the arms and resources of some great Empire, or it can never remain at peace.

It may be of interest to close this résumé of the history
Jerusalem by comparing the route taken by General Allen
with those taken by previous soldiers in their conquests
Judæa. The routes taken by the British have already be
fully described. In only one known case, that of the Fi
Crusade, had Judæa been successfully invaded before by
invader who had not previously made himself master of
least three of her borders.[1] The attempt at a swift ru
across one border made by Cestius Gallus, ended in a failu
which was only wiped out four years later after the Roma
under Vespasian and Titus, had first overrun Galilee a
Samaria and mastered the strongholds round the Judæ
borders. This was the policy followed, a thousand yea
later, by Saladin.

The upland of Judæa has almost never been invaded fro
the barren waterless south.[1] David, operating from Hebro
must have approached Jerusalem from the south, but he w
already in possession of the Judæan plateau. The origi
attempt of the Israelites to enter the country from the sou
was checked, and they subsequently crossed the Jordan a
entered Judæa through Jericho from the east. The Phi
tines must have come up by the passes from the west. Sen
cherib did not approach Jerusalem himself, but it was wh
warring against Egypt at Lachish (Tel el Hesi on the Mariti
Plain) that he sent his arrogant message to Jerusalem; a
it was on the Plain that his victorious army, infected by
plague from Egypt, melted away as by a miracle. Egypt
his objective, not Judæa. Nebuchadnezzar may have invad
Judæa from the north, but it is more probable that he a
came up from the west, after first making himself master
the Maritime Plain. Pompey was returning from his expe
tion in Arabia when he invaded, so he entered from the ea
ascending the Judæan plateau by way of Jericho and Beth
Herod invaded from the north.

[1] G. A. Smith.

In the Christian era, Cestius Gallus made his disastrous
expedition by the Valley of Ajalon, Beth-horon and Gibeon.
Titus, after the surrounding country had been subjugated,
moved his army up to Jerusalem by Gophna (Jufna) and
Bethel, and so through Bireh, from the north-west and north.
The Moslems, in 637, first captured Damascus; subsequently they approached Jerusalem across the Jordan.
The First Crusaders came through Asia Minor and won
a decisive victory at Antioch; thence they came southward along the coast, through Ramleh, and up the Valley
of Ajalon, their advance through the mountains being unopposed. Saladin, by the decisive battle of Hattin, near Tiberias,
made himself master of the surrounding country before closing in upon Jerusalem, which he eventually did from Hebron
(south), from Askalon (west), and from the north. In the
Third Crusade, Richard and his Crusaders came oversea to
Acre; after marching to Ramleh, they tried first to reach the
Holy City up the Valley of Ajalon, and afterwards by the
Vale of Elah, the Wady es Sunt, further to the south, but both
attempts failed.

Many of the invading armies that have swept through Palestine have confined themselves to the great inter-continental
road along the Maritime Plain, and have passed by Jerusalem,
secure upon its plateau. We have seen that this was so with
Sennacherib. This was probably the case with Alexander
the Great, and was undoubtedly so with Napoleon. The
latter defeated the Turks at Gaza and again on the Plain of
Esdraelon. His objective was Syria, but he was foiled by the
action of the British in the siege of Acre. This distraction also
prevented him from making any attempt to reach Jerusalem.

Prior to the arrival of the British, it was seven centuries
since a Christian conqueror had set foot in Jerusalem. But
there was now no gloating of the Cross over the Crescent.
On the contrary, guards of Moslem troops from our Indian
army were placed upon every building sacred to Islam, while

Christian guards were mounted over those sacred to Chri
tianity. Never before had Jerusalem fallen into the hands
conquerors so zealous for the safety of its populace or so co
cerned for the preservation of the city and all that it containe

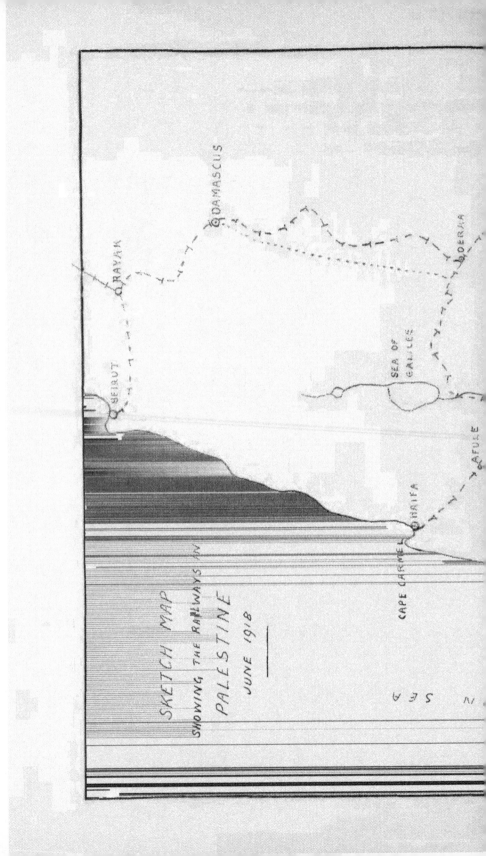

SKETCH MAP
SHOWING THE RAILWAYS IN
PALESTINE
JUNE 1918

DAMASCUS

RAYAK

BEIRUT

SEA OF
GALILEE

DERAA

HAIFA

AFULE

CAPE CARMEL

IN SEA

CHAPTER XII

JUNCTION STATION AND LUDD

AN interesting task fell to my lot, in the reduction to order
of the chaos existing at Junction Station. This place
had been an important rest camp on the enemy's line of
communications. That the Germans thought they had come
to stay was manifested by the style in which the station and
other buildings had been erected, as well as by the plans
which they had left behind them for intended future development. Most of the buildings, including an up-to-date flour
mill fitted with modern machinery, had been substantially
built with stone. The erection of many additional houses
was clearly contemplated, while the work had already been
put in hand of planting fruit orchards.

The disgusting state in which these premises were left was
indescribable. Rotting carcases of beasts lay all about the
place, while other filth almost surpassed them in stench.
The buildings were infested with flies by day and mosquitoes
by night, while other forms of vermin carried on the good
work throughout the whole twenty-four hours.

A large amount of stores had been left behind and had
fallen into our hands, consisting mainly of grain, flour, and
fodder (tibbin). The enemy had destroyed some of the buildings, smashed up the mill machinery, and set on fire as much
of the corn as possible. This fire lasted for days, until at
length it burned itself out, for it was useless attempting to
save any portion of the grain composing the bonfire.

Before we had so much as taken possession, swarms of

Bedouin came through the premises to loot. Thieving w
them is instinctive. They could not understand why tl
had not a right to help themselves to what the Turks had ab
doned. However, a strong guard was posted at once; th
Bedouin who had taken up their abode on the premises w
evicted; and preparations were made to face a somewl
stormy night. All that night through the crack of ri
resounded. Although the bag next morning proved to
small, yet, for days afterwards, Bedouin kept dropping
at our hospitals with bullet wounds to be dressed, as to
cause of which they could offer no satisfactory explanatic
After this the looting fell off considerably. Nevertheless
certain number of looters, averaging about a dozen a da
were caught and put into the Guard Room. We were gl
of their assistance, as there was much filthy cleaning up
be done, so, fools that came to loot, remained to scaven
Once we had an awkward predicament, for the sergeant
the guard, having confined in the same lock-up some loote
whose detention should be for twenty-four hours, and so
prisoners, whose detention should be for the duration of t
war, could not subsequently tell them apart.

The enemy left here intact an entire Turkish hospital. It w
one of the most picturesque of Eastern sights that anybo
could wish to see. Crowded together in one huge ward were m
of every shade, in variegated costumes, lying on beds wi
coverlets rivalling Joseph's coat of many colours. Unfc
tunately, the hospital was infected, or suspected of infectic
with typhus. Therefore, as soon as the patients and st
had been evacuated, it was set on fire, and the whole hospit
woodwork, tents and all that they contained, ascended
heaven in a great column of smoke. Among the conter
was a nice new camp bedstead. Pending the decision as
the competent military authority in whose custody this shou
be placed, I gave orders for it to be transferred to my quarte
But, strangely enough, each senior officer that arrived co

idered that the competent military authority to take charge
of this bedstead was himself. It must have had at least a
dozen owners by the time that it ascended in smoke. This
hospital also contained one case of sardines. It was wonder-
ful how widely spread became the fame of those sardines.
Every British officer in Palestine seems to have licked his lips
and looked forward to a meal of sardines when he should pass
through Junction Station. Unfortunately, nobody could
find those sardines. But a week later, when the rush
of officers had gone, it was discovered that they had been
appropriated as medical comforts by the R.A.M.C. Now, it
so happened, that none of the patients then arriving were on
a sardine diet, so other measures had to be taken to ensure
that the sardines were not wasted.

As the army went forward, they sent back large numbers
of Turkish prisoners of war. These were collected at Junction Station, where a compound was formed. Such as were
required for labour were temporarily detained, while the
others were marched back under guard to railhead.

During this sojourn, the prisoners were usefully employed
in clearing up the messes which had been left behind, particularly in burying carcases. At one place we found half-a-
dozen dead buffaloes lying half submerged. Before they
could be got at and cleared away it was necessary to drain
off the water. A party of the prisoners were detailed for
this task; a few hours later they were found seriously trying
to drain this water away up-hill. Among the prisoners were
a few officers. In default of other suitable accommodation,
one of them was allowed to live in a room at the Commandant's
house. He displayed great anxiety lest somebody should
touch the disused telephone or other wires, fire a booby trap
possibly left behind by his kind friends, and so blow him to
eternity.

There was not much time to spare for contemplation.
Nevertheless, in this, the Vale of Sorek, I often thought of

Samson and Delilah, and " Mon coeur s'ouvre à ton voix
or, pictured the Ark of the Covenant wend its way past
very door, on a cart drawn by two milch kine, on that wond
ful journey from Ekron to Beth-Shemesh.

There was plenty of work to be done, in reducing chaos
order, in protecting much valuable property, in meeti
the requirements of thousands of passing troops, and
spreading, as it were, the spawn for this mushroom town.
had been an important place under Turkish administrati
It promised, under the British régime, to become the m
important railway centre in Palestine. Consequently, schem
of water supply, sanitation, and town planning had to
evolved and installed immediately, hospitals opened in
most appropriate buildings, spaces set apart for campi
grounds for all classes of troops and animals, huge dun
and supply dumps respectively, railway sidings laid do
and cemeteries opened both for Christians and for Mahomeda
while roads had to be improved and sign-boards set up in
directions.

Many and diverse were the arrivals and departures in
course of one busy week. Foremost came the fighting troo
of the 21st Corps, the 75th and 54th Divisions, followed la
by those of the 20th Corps, the 60th and 74th Divisio
With them arrived field ambulances, which took possess
of the best of the buildings and converted them into h
pitals. Companies of Royal Engineers arrived, and travell
workshops staffs of the Ordnance Department, and both
these lost no time in opening their workshops. Enorm
supply dumps were formed and camel convoys, miles lo
arrived with supplies. The camels were specially inco
siderate, and would select awkward spots, like cross-roa
at which to lie down and die. They were welcome to
if only they could and would have first made adequate arran
ments for their own obsequies. A battalion of British W
Indians that arrived, aroused both sympathy and amuseme

They had marched through torrential rain and arrived soaked to the skin. In spite of a warning as to what they might expect, they rushed for shelter into some of the buildings which had not yet been disinfected; but their exit was even faster than their entrance, and they preferred the wet and cheerless exterior to being eaten alive within. Scarcely a day's march behind the fighting troops, arrived a thousand or more of the Egyptian Labour Corps. These were immediately set to work on the roads, and such good work did they do that the roads were soon in an excellent condition for mechanical transport. Full of irony was the arrival of several guards and a staff of military police *en route* for Jerusalem. It was believed, at this time, that the fall of Jerusalem was imminent. That Britain's fair name might not be sullied by any foolish misbehaviour, or any still more foolish collection of souvenirs, it was decided that guards should at once be mounted upon the Holy Places in Jerusalem. These guards, Christian and Moslem, collected at Junction Station, ready to march straight into the city; but, when its fall was postponed *sine die*, they had sadly but surely to return to their own regiments. The intention had been to surround Jerusalem with a cordon of British sentries; an order, accordingly, was published that any British soldier found within 5 miles of Jerusalem would be liable to be shot. Our unfortunate British soldiers fighting on Neby Samwil, which was within the prescribed distance, readily endorsed that sentiment, though scarcely in the sense implied by the authorities.

Of all activities at this time of industry, none were greater than those of the railway development companies of the Royal Engineers. The Turkish line had been destroyed in several places and the rolling stock much damaged. Nevertheless, repairs were put in hand immediately, leaky engines were made water-tight, damaged trucks and coaches were made fit to travel, and, within a very short space of time, there was a train running each way between Junction Station

and Deir Sineid. As being the services of primary importanc
the first trains were confined to the bringing up of ammun
tion and the taking down of wounded. The captured rollin
stock was limited, and so the number of trains was painfull
restricted. Fortunately, this narrow gauge line was
similar gauge to certain light railways in Egypt, and rollin
stock from those lines was brought up with all convenien
speed. Moreover, two quite new engines, said to have bee
originally destined for this line but captured at sea durin
the early days of the war, were hurried up and put into con
mission. New constructional work was also put in hand a
once, including an embankment for continuing the line north
wards across the bed of the Wadi Surar (Sorek), the origin
steel girder bridge having unfortunately been destroye
The fate of the bridges here was similarly unfortunate. Th
railway bridge, which should have been blown up before,
as to prevent the escape of the Turkish trains, was only d
stroyed after they had got away; and so the destruction
this bridge proved of great hindrance to us, but caused
inconvenience whatever to the enemy. The other bridg
across the wadi was a timber bridge, which carried the roa
As this bridge was insecure and required strengthening,
party of military police were posted upon it to stop all traff
from crossing it through the night. Seized with a brain wav
they lit a fire upon the centre of the bridge. This expedie
proved so successful, that it not only stopped the traffic f
that night, but for all time. When morning came, it w
discovered that they had burnt away the bridge itself, and
new bridge had to be constructed.

An armoured train was improvised from such trucks as we
available, the sides being sandbagged and a Lewis gu
mounted in front. With this, the railway line was patroll
towards Jerusalem for some miles, until destroyed bridg
made further progress impossible. The result of this reco
naissance showed that trains could run for some distance alo

is line, and ammunition trains were pushed forward accord-
gly.

When I left Junction Station to rejoin the fighting troops,
was well on the high road to importance and fame. This,
owever, never matured. It was to the policy of railway
nstruction that this place owed its primary existence; it
as to an extension of that policy that it looked for its future
velopment; it was through a change in that policy that its
ory soon afterwards departed.

The original intention had been to adapt to our use the
urkish railway system, merely broadening the gauge. In that
se, our own broad gauge line from Kantara, which, imme-
ately on the fall of Gaza, had been brought through to Deir
neid, would have been continued along the route of the
urkish line from Deir Sineid to Junction Station. The first
onths of working this Turkish line, still in its narrow gauge
ndition as captured, did not afford a promising outlook.
hese were months of torrential and persistent rain. The
untry became a quagmire. Landslips along the permanent
ay, and the washing away of culverts, became of such fre-
ent occurrence, that it was decided to abandon this por-
on of this line altogether. Committed, therefore, to no pre-
termined route, the engineers were left with the whole coun-
y open to them to choose a course for their new trunk rail-
ay to the north. They chose a line much nearer the coast,
d approximately followed the border line between the
rtile plain and the sand dunes from Deir Sineid as far north
Yebna, thence bearing north-east towards Ramleh and Ludd.
is had the effect of making the future railhead at Ludd.
Situate at the cross-roads where the Valley of Ajalon de-
uches upon the Plain, and the ancient route from Jerusalem
Jaffa crosses the yet more ancient route from Egypt and
za to Acre and Damascus, the neighbourhood of Ramleh
d Ludd has for many centuries been the site of an important
wn. In Biblical days it was Ludd; in Crusading days it

was Ramleh. The towns are but a couple of miles apa
And so it came about that now, once again, this spot becad
the great traffic junction of Palestine.

As time passed on, and as, through the spring and sumn
of 1918, we held a line across Palestine to the north of a
covering Jerusalem and Jaffa, railway development proceed
apace, being focussed on Ludd. In spite of the difficult
of railway engineering in the mountains, the broad gauge li
was carried from Ludd through Junction Station right up
Jerusalem. Well-constructed narrow gauge lines were la
down between Ludd and Jaffa, and between railhead a
various distributing centres close behind the front line. T
line from Junction Station to Beersheba was changed fro
narrow to broad gauge and extended to Rafa. Thereaft
the line was double from Kantara to Rafa. From Rafa, o
single line went forward, by Belah, Gaza and Yebna, to Lud
while another single line went forward to Ludd by way
Beersheba and Junction Station. The advantages of a doul
line system north of Rafa were thus secured at times of pre
sure by working the full freight trains forward to Ludd v
Gaza and Yebna, and working the trains of returned empt
back again by way of Beersheba.

Ludd developed apace. Soon were seen all the evidend
and activities of a great advanced base and distributing centi
Huge ordnance and supply dumps arose, workshops and depd
were to be seen on all sides, a great bakery was installed a
even a mineral-water factory. The importance of Ludd i
eclipsed the quondam glory of Belah, and came nearer
rivalling that of Kantara.

To an Englishman, the chief interest of Ludd lies in its bei
the place of martyrdom and burial of St. George. Was
not appropriate that the victorious British armies in Palesti
should have been provided and fed from beside the very tor
of their own Patron Saint ?

CHAPTER XIII

THE JORDAN

JERUSALEM having surrendered on the 9th December, the enemy lay round about in an encircling line on the north and east. The first thing to be done was to make good our hold upon the city. Accordingly, a series of minor operations took place, with the object of clearing the enemy from any points of vantage that he held and driving him further from the city.

On the night of the 26/27th December, determined counterattacks were delivered by the Turks. They attacked the 3rd Division at points east of Jerusalem, and the 60th to the north, their principal objective being Tel el Ful, a conspicuous hill 3 miles east of Neby Samwil, from which Jerusalem and the intervening ground could be overlooked. On the morning of the 28th, a lull occurred in the fighting, followed by an attack of unexpected strength against the whole front. The successes gained by this attack were short-lived. A counterattack by the 74th and 10th Divisions, further to the left, now made itself felt. This was launched against the enemy's reserves, and thus deprived the enemy of the initiative. The Turkish attack being spent, a general advance northward. took place, not, however, without further heavy fighting. Pursuing our advantage, we further advanced our line on the 30th, and occupied a line from Beitior (Bethel), 2 miles northeast of Bireh, to Jameh and Ras Kerker, 7 miles west, northwest of Bireh. Bireh, which had been our objective in November, was, at last, securely in our possession. The Turkish

109

attempt to recapture Jerusalem had ended in crushing defe

Throughout the winter months the weather was misera
wet, and the troops in Palestine, whether engaged in act
operations or merely holding the line, suffered intense d
comfort. The mails brought us letters from our friends
home, saying how much they envied us who were spendi
Christmas in the Holy Land. But those who were up t
line spent Christmas Day soaked to the skin in a gale of wi
and rain, while their Christmas dinner consisted of half-rations
bully beef and biscuit. They were wishing themselves anywh
else upon this earth. The appalling weather conditions ma
it impossible to get more than the bare necessities of life f
ward from railhead, and tons of Christmas luxuries sent fr
England through Egypt lay soaked and rotting in dumps
Deir Sineid.

January was much too wet for operations in this countr
In February, however, General Allenby determined on t
capture of Jericho. The country from round Jerusal
slopes down, as we have seen, very abruptly to Jericho and t
Jordan Valley. Precipitous slopes, rocky ridges and narr
ledges, confined the advance to definite lines on which t
enemy could concentrate fire. The advance began on t
19th, and, by the evening of the 20th, the 60th Division h
reached a line 4 miles west of the cliffs overlooking Jeric
In the meantime, the mounted troops were working on t
right or south of the infantry, towards the commanding po
tion of Neby Musa, near the north-west corner of the De
Sea. This advance was held up at the last wadi which w
directly overlooked by, and subjected to, a heavy fire fr
Neby Musa. Other mounted troops, further to the rig
discovered a way down to the Jordan Plain, where they w
firmly established by dusk. That night the Turks withdre
and our mounted troops, moving up the Plain, entered Jeric
on the morning of the 21st.

There are two or three routes between Jericho and t

summit of the Judæan plateau. That by which the British had now come down was not the route followed by Joshua and the Israelites. They, on the other hand, ascended by a route farther north, through Mukhmas (Michmash) and Beitin (Bethel), thus reaching the summit near Bireh. The route followed by the pilgrims was that of the main road, which hereafter became the main line of supply of the forces operating in this direction.

Having secured Jericho and the low country beyond as far as the Jordan, operations were now commenced with the object of pushing the enemy northwards, and clearing him from another substantial portion of Palestine. This would, at the same time, broaden the base for future operations which were contemplated across the River Jordan.

Operations on a large scale were commenced on March 9th. Both the 20th and 21st Corps were engaged. We will, however, consider here only the operations of the 20th Corps, leaving those of the 21st until a subsequent chapter. The reader is already familiar with the type of country, which resembled that between Jerusalem and Jericho. The downward slopes were exceptionally steep, in places precipitous. The slopes were swept by machine-gun and rifle fire, and the beds of the wadis were enfiladed. The ascent on the far side was steeply terraced. Men had alternately to hoist and pull each other up under fire, and finally to expel the enemy from the summits in hand-to-hand fighting. Under these conditions no rapid advance could be looked for.

The 60th Division, by night, crossed the Wadi el Auja, north of Jericho (not to be confused with the wadi of the same name to the north of Jaffa). This Division seized a position astride the Beisan— Jericho road. The 53rd Division captured Tel-Asur, a conspicuous landmark among a mass of high hills, which mountain the enemy tried repeatedly, but in vain, to recover. Farther to the left, a counter-attack was repulsed by the 10th Division. At the conclusion of the operations, the high ground covering the approaches to the Jordan by the Jericho-Beisan Road had been secured, and also, farther west, linking up with the 21st Corps, the high ground stretching across the hills of Mount Ephraim.

We come now to the passage of the River Jordan and the operations in Eastern Palestine. It will be remembered, from what has already been written,[1] that active operations were in progress about this time between the Turks south-east of the Dead Sea and our Arab allies, the troops of the King of the Hejaz. The Turkish line of communications ran down the Hejaz Railway through eastern Palestine, temptingly near our forces at Jericho. It will also be remembered,[2] that the Jordan Valley, and ascent therefrom into the hills of Eastern Palestine are unique. It would therefore have been difficult or impossible to cut the Turks' Hejaz communications by maintaining a permanent garrison astride the railway, such garrison being based on Jericho with an extremely vulnerable line of communications across the valley. It was thought, however, that much useful service might be rendered to the Arabs if a raiding force were to cross the Jordan and destroy the railway in the neighbourhood of Amman.

The country between the Jordan and Amman offered many obstacles to our advance. There were the marshes of the Jordan Valley to be crossed, ridges of clay to be surmounted, scrub to be negotiated, followed by an ascent of 3,500 feet. The metalled road to Amman crosses the Jordan at the Ghoraniyeh Bridge, and reaches the hills at Shunet Nimrin. It then winds up a wadi to Es Salt, whence it strikes due eastward to Amman.

The operations commenced in the latter part of March. No serious obstacle was encountered until the crossings of the Jordan were reached. A small party was sent in motor-boats across the Dead Sea to dispose of any enemy who might be in the district to the north-east of the Dead Sea, but the met with few traces of the enemy. The enemy had destroyed the bridge at Ghoraniyeh early in the month. Other means had therefore to be devised for effecting a crossing. " Jordan overfloweth all his banks all the time of harvest." On the 28th March, owing to heavy rain, the river rose 9 feet. Floods had, therefore, to be contended with. The current is at all times rapid, and the banks, on account of the floods, are boggy and difficult for the approach of transport. On the night of the 21st/22nd March, the main crossings of the river were attempted, both at Ghoraniyeh, and a few miles further south at Hajlah, where the Pilgrim Road from Jerusalem reaches the Jordan. At the former point three attempts to swim the river were made, under fire, by men with ropes attached to their bodies, but in each case the swimmers were carried away by the strong current and found it impossible to reach the opposite bank. Then a punt was launched, but this was no sooner launched than it was swept away. The attempt was commenced in the bright moonlight, but was much hampered by enemy fire. It was renewed after the moon had gone down, but then it was impossible to find the easiest route or to negotiate the current in the dark. Farther down stream, however, the efforts met with better fortune. A small party succeeded in swimming across in the dark and landing on the left bank. These towed a rope behind them, by which, after landing, they hauled across light rafts. The crossing by the raft-loads of men had to be carried out in the face of some hostile fire. Portions of the scrub had been set on fire by the enemy, and these fires to some extent lit up the rafts as they were being pulled across. By daylight, 300 men had been got across, and a small bridge-head established. A barrel bridge was without delay constructed by the Engineers. Very little progress could be made that day as the scrub was infested with enemy machine guns. On the following night, however, a push was made, and the bridge-head enlarged to a width of 500 yards. That night the Engineers constructed a steel pontoon bridge, and an entire cavalry regiment was passed over by dawn. The cavalry soon cleared away the enemy not only from Hajleh, but also from in front of Ghoraniyeh. Bridges were built now at Ghoraniyeh and the passage of the river assured.

Having successfully crossed the Jordan, the force pushed on eastwards across the low country, meeting with some opposition. Eventually we reached Shunat Nimrin. The enemy retreating up the Es Salt road were bombed and machine-gunned by our aircraft. Part of our force, following on their heels, entered Es Salt on the 25th, while, on the 26th, our mounted troops occupied Amman. The railway to the south of the station was successfully cut, but north of Amman the cutting was not complete. Consequently, the enemy were able to receive considerable reinforcements. Before Amman could be attacked in strength some 4,000 Turks were in position covering the viaduct and tunnel, while 2,000 more were moving on Es Salt from the north. Five miles of railway line were however, destroyed, while much other damage was done to the railway line. But, in view of the strength of the enemy and the difficulties of our communications (we had only been able to bring forward mountain-artillery), our force withdrew.

The raid had not entirely fulfilled its object, but much good work had been done, and it had materially assisted Sheri Faisal with his Hejaz troops in his operations further south against Maan.

Our force returning from Eastern Palestine did not abandon the hardly-won eastern bank of the Jordan. Bridge-heads were retained. The Turks, however, became aggressive, and on the 11th April, attacked our bridge-head at Ghoraniyeh. They were repulsed from here and driven back to Shunet Nimrin, which they strongly garrisoned.

On the 30th April another raid was made across the Jordan. This time our infantry attacked the Shunet Nimrin position, while the cavalry, intending to cut off the garrison, moved

und the flank and reached Es Salt. But a strong Turkish
rce, crossing the Jordan from the Nablus area at Jisr ed
amieh, drove back the cavalry, who lost nine guns in their
tirement. This raid had been planned to co-operate with
e Beni Sakr Arabs. Their promised assistance did not
aterialize, and the whole force was brought back to the cross-
gs of the Jordan.

Thenceforth, until the sweep of the following September
e Jordan river and bridge-heads remained our front line.

CHAPTER XIV

THE WADI DEIR BALLUT

IN the last chapter we saw how, after the capture of Jer
salem, the 20th Corps proceeded to improve the line o
the right. We will now follow the operations of the 21st Cor
on the left.

The first operation of importance was that carried out by tl
52nd Division on the extreme left. On the night of tl
20th/21st December, 1917, crossings, partly by fording al
partly by rafts, were effected over the Wadi Auja, a few mil
to the north of Jaffa. The high ground overlooking the wa
from the north was rushed before dawn, and a line was co
solidated which effectually deprived the enemy of all observ
tion from the north over the Valley of the Wadi Auja. Inc
dentally, the distance between the enemy and Jaffa w
increased from 3 to 8 miles. This safeguarded Jaffa and i
harbour, and the main Jaffa—Jerusalem road. Furth
adjustments of the line were made, including the capture
Rantieh on the railway and El Tine and Bornat to the rigl
which gave commanding views over the forward country a
increased elbow room to the troops covering Ludd and Ramle

As the result of these operations the line ran, at the begi
ning of March, approximately as follows. The 60th Divisi
on the right had reached the Jordan, our line running alo
that river as far north as the Wadi Auja and then bendi
westwards. On their left came the 53rd Division, a little to t
north of Bireh, and on their left again the 10th Division co
pleted the front of the 20th Corps. They joined up the 75
Division, whose frontage ran from Midieh (the Modin of t

116

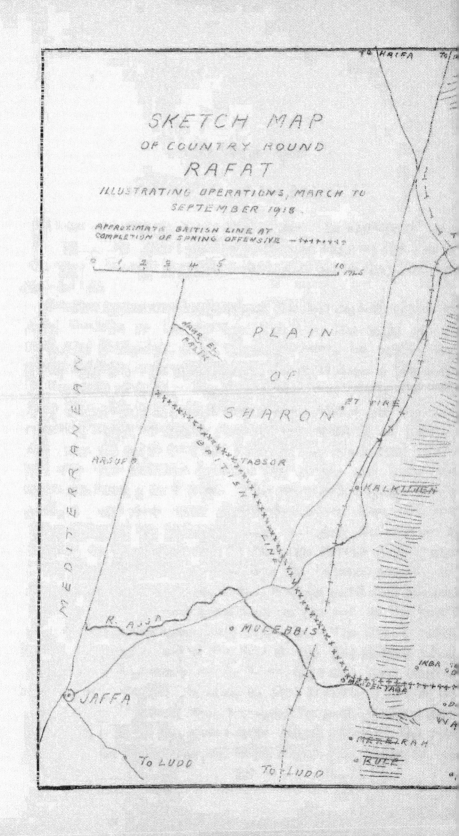

SKETCH MAP
OF COUNTRY ROUND
RAFAT
ILLUSTRATING OPERATIONS, MARCH TO
SEPTEMBER 1918.

APPROXIMATE BRITISH LINE AT
COMPLETION OF SPRING OFFENSIVE ━┼╌┼┼┼┼┼┼

0   1   2   3   4   5   10   MLS

PLAIN

OF

SHARON

NAHR EL
FALIK

PT. TIRE

ARSUFR

TABSOR

KALKILIEH

R. AUJA

MULEBBIS

IKBA

MEDEL TABA

JAFFA

WA

MER EL RAH

TO LUDD

TRUER

TO LUDD

TO HAIFA

accabees) through Kibbiah to the foot-hills at Et Tireh;
om here the 54th Division extended across the Plain; while
e 52nd Division held the sector close to the sea, a little to
e north of the other Wadi Auja.

Except for occasional rains, our soldiering in the 75th
vision sector, throughout February and the early part of
arch, was campaigning *de luxe*. The enemy had gone right
ck to the line of the Wadi Deir Ballut, leaving a No Man's
nd in front of us about 4 miles across. He held advanced
sts a mile or two in front of our line, but his guns had been
ken well back out of range. We therefore enjoyed immunity
th from sniping and shelling, and could move about in front
our line without anxiety, even in broad daylight. The
servation posts that we occupied commanded extensive views
ross No Man's Land, and we should have had early intima-
n had there been any considerable hostile movement.

We thus had opportunities for training, and preparing
rselves for the next forward push. The whole battalion
s put through a course of musketry. The forward slopes
our position provided an admirable field firing range, with
No Man's Land for the stray bullets to spend themselves
on. How it must have made the Turk itch to see men lying
out in platoons in the open before his very eyes, and how he
ist have longed to have had a gun within range, and to have
spersed us with a few rounds of shrapnel. We also insti-
ted a very successful shooting-gallery. In the front line beer
s seldom procurable, though much appreciated. Such as we
re able to obtain from the canteen was taken to the rifle
nge. An empty bottle was set up 200 yards in front of the
er and a full one behind him. If he hit the former he became
titled to the contents of the latter. Each man was entitled
one free shot, and as many more as he liked at a cost of a
nny each. The result was, that, at a very nominal cost to
canteen funds, the individual shooting of the battalion
nsiderably improved.

Aerial activity was interesting. We soon became acc[us]tomed to the distinctive hum of the Hun machines flying h[igh] above us, followed by the barking of our "Archies." Then [we] could trace the track of the planes across the sky by the [line] of white smoke puffs left by our bursting archy shells. Ar[chy] seldom reckons to get a direct hit on a plane, but, by the [ex]penditure of quantities of ammunition, he makes the [Hun] fly too high to see anything of value or to drop bombs w[ith] much hope of success. More tangible results were obtai[ned] by our fighting planes, which engaged the Hun in the air. [A] pretty little fight took place a thousand feet or so above [our] heads, between two of our planes and a couple of Huns. A[fter] preliminary circling and manœuvring for place, during wh[ich] one Hun machine discreetly went all out for home, one of [our] planes swooped straight on to the remaining Hun, pourin[g a] burst of Lewis gun fire into the pilot and observer at sh[ort] range. Badly wounded, the Hun pilot turned his mach[ine] full speed for home. But our other plane, which had retai[ned] its altitude, hovered over him, headed him off from hom[e] and shepherded him down on to the Plain, where he w[as] forced to land and was captured. On another occasion, [we] were puzzled to see a Hun plane, returning from our lin[e] pitch in enemy territory, and, though unattacked, go up [in] smoke and flame. Subsequent reports furnished an expla[na]tion. The Hun pilot had descended without being very s[ure] of his whereabouts. The Turks, mistaking him for a Britis[h] opened fire upon him with a machine gun. Thereup[on] believing himself to be in hostile territory, the pilot burnt [his] machine and surrendered—to his own friends !

Campaigning de luxe ! The wild flowers did all that lay [in] their power to add to the luxury. The warm sun of Febru[ary] and March, following the drenching rain of the winter, p[ro]duces in Palestine a profusion of beautiful flowers that is pr[ob]ably surpassed nowhere. The country-side was liter[ally] carpeted with choice flowers of sweet smell and varied colo[ur]

To mention but a few—there were red. white, and blue anemones; cyclamen, white, pink and mauve; aromatic herbs; poppies and corn-flowers; scarlet tulips; pink phlox; blue irises, velvety arum lilies, black and crimson, tall, stately hollyhocks. And the catalogue is scarce begun. Truly a floral Paradise!

Early in March came rumours of a forward move. The nominal pretext was an improvement of our line. Other motives may possibly have been influencing the higher authorities, such as keeping the initiative in our hands, fostering an aggressive spirit, and feeling the strength of the enemy with a view to subsequent operations on a larger scale.

Almost opposite Jaffa the central range of Judæan hills is cleft by a great gorge. Starting at a point on the edge of, and almost overlooking the Jordan Valley, it runs approximately due east and west, with many turns and even hairpin bends, until it debouches on the Plain at Mejdel Yaba, thence forming a main tributary of the River Auja. In the days of the Maccabees this gorge formed the frontier between the Jews and the Samaritans. This gorge is the Wadi Deir Ballut. The sides of this wadi are at all points steep, at some precipitous, presenting in places an almost sheer drop of several hundred feet. The bed of the wadi is from a hundred to a couple of hundred yards wide and the surface level. Thus the Wadi Ballut formed an admirable defensive line for the Turk; after it had passed into our hands, it provided us with an admirable line of communication.

The Turk, at this time, held the line of the Wadi Ballut with such advanced posts as could deny to our patrols all access to the wadi. Available information about the wadi was thus restricted to reports and maps, and was none too ample or reliable. The intermediate country consisted of approximately flat " merjs," intersected with wadis, and dotted about with hills, villages, and other features of tactical importance. At this time of the year it somewhat resembled the general

I

appearance of Exmoor. For several days prior to the advance patrols were sent out into No Man's Land, that as much as possible might be ascertained about, and as many as possible be made familiar with, the terrain over which we had to operate.

On the 12th March, the whole 75th Division, in co-operation with the Divisions on its flanks, moved forward. The operations of this day were perhaps little more than minor operations, certainly not one of the decisive battles of the war, although their effect in drawing reinforcements to Palestine may have had far-reaching results in other zones such as Mesopotamia. Nevertheless, as they formed such a pretty field day, so like our manœuvres at home, I venture upon a short description, in the hope that it may be of interest to those whose soldiering experience has been confined to the home front. There was no horrid barbed wire to contend with, nor gas. There were not even trenches, for the Turks' defence work here consisted only of stone walls, technically known as sangars. During the commencing stages we were not even shelled.

Shortly after dawn, our heavy artillery opened the ball by shelling the advanced posts of the enemy. At seven o'clock the whole line moved forward. Our first objective, a prominent knoll, was 4,000 yards away, and no previous opposition was expected. Having assumed the appropriate formation before crossing the crest, we moved forward in " artillery " formation, that is to say, in lines of platoons in file. For the non-military reader, it should be explained that this is the formation in which troops are considered least vulnerable against artillery or distant rifle and machine-gun fire. Great care was taken to ensure that direction was maintained, an officer with compass being specially detailed for this purpose, and that touch was not lost with the units on either flank. A battery of field artillery had been detailed to support the advance of this battalion ; the forward observation officer went forward

with the infantry; the battery, less one section temporarily
left behind, moved forward close behind us to a previously
selected position from which the Deir Ballut Ridge would be
within easy range. A section of machine gunners moved
forward close behind the leading companies. In a fold of
the ground, some 1,400 yards short of the first objective, the
infantry shook out into lines of skirmishers. They continued
their advance, and occupied the knoll which was their first
objective without opposition.

Meanwhile, after a concentrated bombardment on the left,
the first and second of the enemy's forward posts were captured without serious opposition; it appeared probable that
these had been occupied mainly for observation and that his
principal resistance was to be offered upon the Ballut Ridge.

After a short halt on the first objective, to conform to the
time-table, we moved forward again in the same formation
against our second objective, a ridge which seemed to overlook the Wadi Deir Ballut. We still met with no opposition,
until we put our heads up over the ridge, when we were greeted
with a torrent of bullets from machine guns posted on the
opposite side of the wadi. This wadi, it will be remembered,
was to us *terra incognita*. The first thing to be done therefore
was to make a hurried reconnaissance, and decide on the best
method of getting down and across. It was found that the
descent was almost a sheer precipice, and that we had not
one but two wadis to cross, a smaller tributary wadi, scarcely
marked on the map, forming, in fact, a rather serious obstacle.
Carrying out such a reconnaissance, upon a forward slope,
under machine gun fire from across the wadi, was none too
easy. It had been intended that the leading company, which
took the ridge, should at once open covering fire across the
wadi, whilst the company following should pass through them
and cross the wadi under cover of their fire. However, the
difficulty of taking up suitable positions for seeing the target,
and the extremity of the range (about 1,500 yards), made it

inadvisable for the infantry to fire. But the machine gunn
attached to us soon brought their machine guns into actio
while our artillery f.o.o. took up a position on the ridge fro
which he could fire his guns to good effect.

About this time, away to our left, developed the attack
Mejdel Yaba. This village occupies a commanding positi
overlooking the Plain, and, in Crusading days, was a fortre
That phase of the battle proved an artillery action pure a
simple. The whole artillery of a Division, with several heav
added, was concentrated on that luckless spot. It afforded
spectacle not soon to be forgotten. When the infantry arrive
they found the work all over ; the Turks had all been kill
by the bombardment or fled from the village, most of the latt
having been cut off and killed by our machine guns. Befo
leaving, the Turks had taken the precaution of interviewi
the headman of the village and cutting his throat.

To return to our own corner of the picture, under cover
the fire of our own artillery and machine guns the first co
pany went forward. Slipping down that mountain side was
veritable case of running the gauntlet. But, once the botto
of the first wadi was reached, some cover was afforded for
breather. Almost in front of us, on the far ridge, lay t
village of Deir Ballut, on which the enemy evidently intend
to base their strongest resistance. On our left, the infant
were making a good pace ; on the right they were held up, b
seeing us going forward, they pushed forward too, so th
pressure might be maintained all along the line. The ene
had organized his defences and placed his machine guns wi
great skill. The slopes of the wadi were too steep for go
shooting straight down the slope. So he had taken full adva
tage of the curves and hairpin bends of the wadi to place
machine guns in position sweeping the spurs and giving ea
other mutual support. Our leading company lost no ti
in getting to work. They dumped their packs and set o
at once to storm the ridge. Meanwhile, our infantry advanci

the left, had taken some of the enemy machine guns in
nk, forcing them to withdraw, which materially assisted the
vance of the leading company. And so the leading com-
ny, closely followed by companies in support, established
lf on the Ridge.

The fiercest of the fighting, however, was yet to come. A
at burst of machine-gun fire caused the leading platoon to
e cover under one of the terraces. Hence they were at
e led forward again. The Turks now delivered a strong
unter-attack. Seeing this, the leading platoon dashed for-
rd with their bayonets, led by the company cook, and the
rks were put to flight. The Lewis-gunners caught them as
ey were getting away and effectually quenched all desire
renew the counter-attack. Then the company pushed
ward, and, ignoring the village of Deir Ballut, with its
chine guns tried to get across the line of retreat from the
lage. Seeing this, the Turks evacuated Deir Ballut, and,
der cover of machine guns posted on the further ridges,
se left alive made good their escape. That evening found
in undisputed possession of Deir Ballut Ridge from beyond
village of Deir Ballut down to the Plain at Mejdel Yaba.

CHAPTER XV

THE MOUNTAINS OF EPHRAIM

W E now found ourselves well established in the Mou
tains of Ephraim, and at no great distance from t
enemy. After the taking of Ballut Ridge he had dropp
back, and was soon seen to be entrenching and sangaring
new line from 2,000 to 4,000 yards further north. Bal
Ridge had been fixed as our final objective. Had there be
possible roads by which guns and supplies could have be
brought forward, an immediate pursuit or attack of the ene
might have proved successful ; but, with such hopeless co
munications, deliberate action was a necessity.

After the Ridge had been captured, the enemy were pursu
with all the fire from rifles, machine guns and artillery th
could be brought to bear. Cavalry, or even infantry purs
across these mountains was out of the question. An outp
line was established and the troops settled down to a wet a
somewhat cheerless night. The mountain sides had been
steep that it had been impossible to bring up any comfor
and even the camels bearing the reserve supply of ammuniti
could only be got forward with extreme difficulty. Exce
for shelling, we were left unmolested during the night and ne
morning, which gave us the opportunity of constructing sa
gars, making tracks for the pack transport animals, and gen
ally making ourselves more comfortable. Patrols were se
forward, and it was ascertained that the country to our imn
diate front was clear of the enemy.

The effect of this advance was to draw down reinforcemei

to this sector, and to divert into Palestine reserves of Turkish troops ; these came largely from the Caucasus, where the total collapse of Russia had set many good Turkish troops at liberty. There was evidence that these troops had been intended for an offensive campaign in Mesopotamia. It is probable, therefore, that this advance, indirectly, yet substantially, contributed to the defence of Mesopotamia, for the Turkish offensive in that area never materialized. Two or three German Divisions came down to stiffen up the Turks, and from this time forward the resistance which we had to face became unmistakebly hardened. The days of campaigning *de luxe* had gone for ever. Before our "archies" could get forward, the Hun aeroplanes had very much their own way, and, flying low, dropped bombs and machine-gunned us in a manner that was most uncomfortable. Enemy artillery shelled any movements on the forward slope, and brought a searching fire to bear, in the hope of damaging our bivouac areas behind the crest. The manner in which the front line was held in the mountains by the Turks as well as by ourselves, was as follows. Strong sangars were constituted on the forward slope of a hill or ridge. By day these were occupied only by a small and well-protected observation party, at times supplemented with a Lewis gun team ; and the remainder of the garrison were withdrawn behind the crest to bivouac areas on the reverse slope. At dusk, the garrison moved forward and manned the front line, being withdrawn again during the half-light of dawn. Thus the hostile artillery could never see a target upon which to fire. Searching a steep reverse slope with guns is almost impossible while, even with howitzers, unless observation can be obtained, an enormous amount of ammunition has to be used to secure any result.

Meanwhile, preparations proceeded apace. With a genius little short of that which has made roads across the Himalayas and the Alps, roads were soon engineered down and up the steep sides of the Wadi, so that within two or three weeks it was possible to bring guns across the Wadi and over the Ballut Ridge. Water supplies, of which excellent springs were discovered in the bed of the wadi, were developed ; later, the cisterns on the hills were closed down to prevent mosquito breeding and malaria.

On the 14th March, the enemy moved forward to counter-attack the Ballut Ridge line, but were caught in close formation by our artillery and the counter-attack never developed. On the 19th, a slight advance was made on our right, which brought the village of Beit Rima (possibly the Ramathaim of the Maccabees) within our line. Another forward move was evidently in the wind and patrolling activity increased all along our line.

A detailed account of one of these patrol incidents may be instructive as affording an example of how such a patrol should be handled. The patrol commander was an experienced soldier who had seen service with almost every battalion of the regiment and in most of the theatres of this war ; his sleeve was covered with wound stripes, and hostile snipers only made him angry.

The orders which he received were to patrol as far as Ikba and to protect some senior officers, who wished to make a reconnaissance and for whose safety he was responsible. He had under his command one platoon, consisting of three sections of riflemen and one of Lewis gunners ; also one other officer to assist.

A glance at the sketch map will show Ballut Ridge, which formed our front line, and Three Bushes Hill, the most forward position held by the enemy. Ikba, or to give it its full name Khurbet Umm el Ikba, thus lay in No Man's Land at no great distance from the enemy. Though standing on a hill and commanding an admirable view of the surrounding country it is overlooked at a range of a mile from Three Bushes Hill and also at shorter distances within effective rifle range from the points marked A, B and C, and, to some extent, from the point marked E. F is a lower knoll, commanded from Ikba. Both E and F are commanded from A.

Moving forward before dawn, the patrol commander led his patrol forward down the Wadi Ikba. Each section was kept apart, and moved forward in single file under its own commander. To each section commander were given precise orders as to the position which he was to occupy, what he was to do, and when he was to withdraw. One section moved down the ridge on the right of the wadi, and took up a position at the point B. One section, with the junior officer, moved first along the wadi bed, and then, while it was still only half light, ascended the left-hand spur and took up a position at A. The Lewis-gun team occupied the hill at C. The remaining section, which had been kept in reserve at the hills about D, now moved forward and occupied Ikba. All being reported clear, the senior officers moved forward, arriving at Ikba just as the daylight became strong enough for them to obtain the forward view of the enemy country which they desired.

An even better view of the country seemed probable from the spur at A. So across there went the officers, including the patrol commander. By the time they arrived, rifle reports were cracking, and the situation was becoming interesting. The reconnaissance finished, the patrol commander gave the senior officers five minutes in which to withdraw, before the expiration of which he would not begin to withdraw his patrol.

Meanwhile, the enemy upon Three Bushes Hill, had espied the party in Ikba, and set out to capture the patrol. Creeping along under cover, they established themselves at the point E. Thence they started to move on to the point F, but came under fire from the section on point A. It became a case of running the gauntlet, but the section were shooting well and dropped their men. The section at Ikba was withdrawing; the enemy, failing to realize that the spur A was occupied, rushed across to A intending to shoot up the wadi at the section withdrawing from Ikba. They were greeted

with a warm reception from the section already at A and beat a
hasty retreat. The section at A now withdrew up the wadi,
covered by the fire of the section still in position at B and by
the Lewis gunners at C. The reserve section from Ikba, who
had been the first to withdraw, had meanwhile taken up another
section in rear, and, under their protection, the section at B
and the Lewis-gunners from C withdrew up the wadi. The
enemy had apparently had enough of it, for the pursuit was
not pressed. A few rounds of shrapnel were fired at us as a
parting present, but no casualties were sustained. This
patrol commander had paid attention to, and illustrated the
soundness of, the cardinal principles of mountain fighting,
namely, the necessity for seizing and piquetting the commanding heights, and the support of the movement of one
party of troops by the fire of other parties already in position.
The plan of using the Lewis gun as a reserve of fire, kept well
back to cover the retirement of the remainder, was undoubtedly sound. Had the commanding heights not been first
secured, it is difficult to see how the patrol could have withdrawn in the face of the enemy without confusion and without
casualty.

On the 27th March the whole line moved forward. The
advance was only intended to be for a depth of about a mile,
in order to secure a better tactical line for defence. None of
the objectives were believed to be held by the enemy. Accordingly, the advance was carried out by night. A full moon,
giving light throughout the night, facilitated the operation.
As soon as daylight was gone, the whole line crept noiselessly
forward, with bayonets fixed ready to meet any possible
opposition with cold steel. Away to our right, the enemy
detected movement, and put down a barrage. But their
firing was somewhat wild; the barrage came down behind the
advancing troops and caused no casualties. On our front
the enemy had not awakened to what was taking place, and
our objectives were attained without molestation. It was

realized that our new positions would be overlooked from the enemy's observation posts on Three Bushes Hill and on Arara, and that, when they saw us by daylight occupying the nearer ridges, they would shell us unmercifully. Accordingly, the remainder of the night was not devoted to sleep, but to the intensive building of sangars on the new defensive line, and the preparations of bivouac areas in such few spots as might be under cover from view and from fire. When morning came, the enemy commenced to shell, but the night had not been wasted, and our fellows had made themselves secure.

This new line was not very comfortable. To such an extent was it overlooked by the enemy that all movement by day was out of the question, and even incinerator fires had for a time to be forbidden. The enemy attacked this new line a few days after it had been taken up. However, our artillery caught the enemy's troops in close order before they had been deployed, and so we experienced no greater inconvenience than a bombardment, doing no great damage. It was not expected that this new line would have to be held for any great length of time. Already preparations were being pushed on for another encounter with the enemy.

CHAPTER XVI

RAFAT

WE have seen, in an earlier chapter, that throughout the campaign in Palestine the left British flank, near the sea, was at all times much in advance of the right. We have already discussed the cause and advantages; there was one distinct disadvantage. As the trend of the country sloped up from the Maritime Plain, the enemy on our right front was on higher ground and had the advantages of observation. If there were a commanding position to our front, and we moved forward and captured it, we found that there were yet other positions beyond, from which that position was itself commanded. Our positions on the Ephraim Mountains along the Ballut Ridge were at this time overlooked from three commanding hills in the possession of the enemy, known as Arara, Rafat, and Three Bushes. Further to the right were the villages of El Kep and Berukin, also on high ground. Owing to the conformation of the country the key of this district was Arara.

In order to improve the general line, and in preparation for a further advance, it was decided to move forward and to capture all these commanding positions. Accordingly, on the morning of the 9th April, the line moved forward. The village of El Kep was a nest of machine guns. After heavy bombardment it was captured after stubborn resistance. Berukin was also captured after sharp fighting, but further progress in this locality was held up. Next day these villages were heavily

130

counter-attacked, and, though they were firmly held, further progress was out of the question.

Meanwhile, a battalion of Somersets had captured Rafat, and a battalion of Dorsets Three Bushes Hill. Enemy shelling now became intense, followed up by counter-attacks, all of which were repulsed.

The intention had been that the Somersets should capture Rafat first and then take Arara, the main objective of these operations. The capture of Three Bushes Hill was necessary to secure Arara and Rafat from reverse fire. But, to enable Arara to be held, it was also necessary to capture other heights to the south-east, notably one called The Pimple. Most of these heights were captured, but, although determined efforts were made, the enemy could not be dislodged from The Pimple. Nevertheless, the Somersets moved forward from Rafat and successfully established themselves upon Arara. Here they were fired at from all sides. They found that Arara was itself commanded from a height called Sheikh Silbih, a thousand or two yards beyond, while the reserve fire from the machine guns on The Pimple soon made their position on Arara untenable. They fell back upon, and firmly established themselves in, their positions at Rafat. One lad, who was left behind in this retirement, had a terrible experience. Wounded in three or four places, he was unable to withdraw with the remainder of his company. He lay out on Arara for three days, after which he was discovered by some Turks. These proceeded to strip him, whereupon he made known to them that he was still alive. They then bayonetted him, and left him for dead. He lay out there for yet another day, now naked, when he was found by a German stretcher-party. These took pity upon him, and removed him to a hospital where he was nursed back to life.

The position on Three Bushes Hill had become interesting. If left in our undisputed possession, it would have rendered the main line of enemy trenches untenable. On the other hand, if the enemy could drive us off, he might from there roll up Rafat and our other positions. He therefore made several determined attempts throughout the day to retake this hill. The position was not altogether unlike that on Spion Kop. Each side clung to the slope immediately below the summit, the forward slope being untenable through shell fire ; our guns were unable to silence the hostile batteries. There was this difference, however, from Spion Kop, for here there was no question at present of withdrawing. The difficulties of bringing supplies, water and ammunition up, and the even greater difficulty of carrying the wounded down a pathless precipice 400 feet high, can be better imagined than described. This work had mostly to be done by night, for our communication line was under enemy observation. The last of the ambulance camels, which were evacuating wounded from the regimental aid post had not crossed the Ballut Ridge and got out of sight before dawn, and were shelled accordingly.

The enemy delivered counter-attacks again in the night ; these also were repulsed. Next morning he changed his tactics. Continuing to shell the back areas, he now pushed up snipers, who established themselves where they could fire at any movement. In so far as the snipers near the summit of the ridge were concerned, a service of counter-sniping was established. But, what was more difficult to deal with, he established snipers on the lower slopes of his own side of the ridge, who could look down upon, and make themselves unpleasant towards, Rafat. Accordingly, it was decided to clear the forward slope.

The Dorsets had now been fighting on the hill for forty-eight hours. Accordingly, on the night of the 10th/11th, they were relieved by an Indian battalion, the Outrans. Just before dawn this battalion moved forward, surprised the Turks, drove them down the hill and consolidated a line along the forward slope, with observation posts and Lewis gunners, withdrawing the remainder of the battalion behind the crest.

The sniping had thus been stopped for the time, and the day was passed in comparative quiet. At dusk, that evening, down came one of the most furious bombardments put down by the enemy in Palestine. Guns from all quarters concentrated on the hill, and practically blotted out the devoted band that were holding the forward line. The bombardment was followed up by a determined counter-attack, but this was repulsed, the battalion of Dorsets being brought back to support the Outrans on the hill.

It was now realized that the only way by which the Arara position could be captured and held, was by a general advance of the line to at least a thousand yards farther to the north, so as to capture The Pimple, Sheikh Subih, and the enemy works beyond Three Bushes. Accordingly, preparations were put in hand, and all was ready for this further advance, when there came—the disaster in France.

The great German offensive in France had commenced on the 21st March, and, a few days later, occurred that great break through which very nearly altered the whole complexion of the war. At first this was not allowed to prejudice the operations in Palestine. But, as the seriousness of the situation in France became realized, no effort was spared to collect more men to fill the gap. Orders were given to cease all further active operations on a large scale in Palestine, and to send to France all the men that could be spared.

Accordingly, there was no alternative but to consolidate, to heavily wire and sangar in upon the line that had been already reached, making such tactical readjustments as were necessary.

It might appear at first sight that the net result of these operations was negative, and that the poor fellows who had given their lives here had died in vain. But this was not so. Rafat was destined to become famous. It was fortified on an almost impregnable scale, thousands of pounds were spent, and a couple of million sand-bags were worked into its defences. A veritable fortress was established which overlooked much of the enemy positions. More than once was this fortress attacked by the Turks, but in vain. It ultimately formed the firm pivot on which was based the great sweep which conquered Palestine.

Feeling between the Turks and the Germans was growing intensely bitter. Germans were not allowed to walk about singly behind the Turkish lines, for fear of assassination. In an attack made by them in the Jordan Valley in July, not only did the Turks fail to move forward in support of the Germans, but they actually fired upon the Germans, when, through lack of that support, they were compelled to retire. It was a case of " a house divided against itself " and it could not therefore hope long to stand.

Active operations on a large scale in Palestine having been stopped, the army was not reorganized. It was a matter of keen regret to many who had followed the fortunes of this campaign since the days of Gaza, that they and their battalions were not to play a part in the final act. The 52nd and the 74th Divisions were withdrawn entirely, their places being taken by the 3rd and 7th Indian Divisions from Mesopotamia. All those remaining, except the 54th, were converted into Indian Divisions, 75 per cent of their battalions being withdrawn and replaced by fresh battalions from India. Those withdrawn were, in some cases, sent to France, in others, broken up and used for reinforcements in the country. Hitherto the army in Palestine had consisted mainly of Territorials. Henceforth it was to consist mainly of Indians.

CHAPTER XVII

THE CROWNING VICTORY

THE Turkish forces in Palestine, in the autumn of 1918, consisted of three armies, the 8th and the 7th, plus one added Division on the west of the Jordan, and the 4th army in the east. All were under the supreme command of the German General, Liman von Sanders.

The line held by the enemy west of the Jordan extended roughly from the sea, south of the Nahr el Falik (some 14 miles north of Jaffa), across western Palestine approximately east, south-east to near Rafat, thence easterly and south-easterly, across the Nablus—Jerusalem Road, and so down to the Jordan Valley. Thus, a portion of his force was entrenched across the Maritime Plain, while the remainder was in the mountains of the Central Range. These mountains of Ephraim and Samaria form a rugged, isolated plateau, which is bounded on the north and east by the low-lying Valleys of Esdraelon and the Jordan. North-west, the mountains continue in a broken chain, till they fall precipitously to the sea at Cape Carmel.

There were two or three routes available to the enemy for supply or retreat, behind the Samaritan plateau. Most important of these was the railway, which, leaving the main Damascus—Hejaz line at Deraa, ran westwards down the Yarmuk Valley to the Jordan, thence through Beisan, and up the Vale of Jezreel and along the Plain of Esdraelon to Haifa. From El Afule, a junction in the middle of the Esdraelon Plain, the south-bound line branched off, and, passing through Jenin

K

(close by Jezreel), wound its way among the mountains up t
Messudieh Station, close to Samaria. Thence a short line ra
on to Nablus, while the main line continued down the slop
of the Wadi Shair to the Maritime Plain, which it reached a
Tul Keram. The advanced enemy bases at Nablus and Tu
Keram were served also by good roads. That from Tul Keram
followed the line of the railway up to a point near Samaria
where it joined the main north-bound road leading from Nablu
down to Jenin and El Afule. From El Afule it would b
possible to go down the Vale of Jezreel (along the road wher
Jehu drove furiously) to Beisan, and thence northward up th
Jordan Valley. But the better road from Jenin and El Aful
leads across the Plain of Esdraelon to Nazareth and Tiberia
and round the northern side of the Sea of Galilee to Damascus
Another road from Nablus leads eastwards, and, droppin
steeply down along the Wadi Fara, leads to the Jordan, which i
crosses by a ford at Jisr ed Damie. The places of tactica
importance on the enemy lines of communication behind hi
advanced bases were, therefore, the railway junctions a
Deraa and El Afule, the ford of Jisr ed Damie, and the towns o
Beisan, Jenin and Nazareth.

The broad outline of General Allenby's plan of operation
was an attack in overwhelming force against the enemy'
positions on the Maritime Plain, followed by a right wheel o
his left flank on a front of 16 miles from Rafat to the sea
thereby rolling up the Turkish line and driving them all int
the Samaritan hills ; meanwhile, his cavalry were to dash fo
the tactical points behind the Turkish line and so close al
enemy lines of retreat.

Some weeks before the date fixed for the commencement o
operations, the several Divisions were by turn withdraw
behind the line and put through a three weeks' course o
intensive training. Then a rearrangement of the line too
place, whereby an overwhelming force was concentrated o
the left. The 60th Division, and most of the cavalry, wer

moved across to the extreme left from the Jordan Valley. Divisions in the line were so rearranged that the line from Rafat to the right was only held thinly, while the garrison of the line from Rafat to the sea was doubled by the addition of three more Divisions, including the 60th on the sea and a French Division at Rafat. All these movements were carried out with the utmost secrecy. The fact that the push was coming along the Maritime Plain was successfully camouflaged, and the enemy led to believe that the push would come up the Jordan Valley. The hotel at Jerusalem was closed, and got in readiness, ostensibly for occupation by G.H.Q. Empty lorries were run up and down the Jordan Valley. Tents were left standing there and dummy-horse lines arranged. Dummy horses were left in the Jordan Valley to convey to enemy aerial observers the impression that cavalry were still there in strength. All the marching towards the Jordan Valley was by day; all the marching towards the Maritime Plain was carried out by night, while by day these troops were hidden in the olive and orange groves that abound on this portion of the Plain. So successful were these ruses, and so complete the surprise, that enemy aerial reconnaissances, made a day before the attack, reported that there was unusual movement in the Jordan Valley and that there was no unusual movement in the coastal sector. The whole of the operations were a triumph of secrecy and of organization.

On the day before the main attack, a small advance was carried out by the right wing just west of the Jordan, occupying El Mugheir. This place is the junction of several roads leading from the west to the east of the Jordan. The object of this preliminary move was to prevent the Turks west of the river escaping by this route to the east, and also to draw the attention of the enemy towards the Jordan Valley and distract from the coastal sector.

By the night of the 18th/19th September, our troops were in position. The Divisions occupying the line from the sea on the left were the 60th, the 7th and the 75th on the Plain the 3rd where Plain and hills meet about Mejdel Yaba, the 54th and the French at Rafat. Thence the line was held by the 10th Division, assisted by a composite force, and, on the extreme right, about the recently captured Mugheir, by the 53rd. Cavalry were concentrated behind the 60th Division ready to dash forward directly the line should be broken.

At 4.30 on the morning of the 19th September, there suddenly opened an intensive bombardment of the enemy's coastal positions, carried out by all the artillery, trench-mortars and machine-guns that could be concentrated in this small sector the navy also co-operating. After ten minutes' bombardment the infantry moved forward and assaulted the enemy's front line positions, which were carried with but little opposition. Thereafter the barrage lifted and crept, being supplemented in places by smoke barrages dropped from aeroplanes. The infantry pushed forward and captured the enemy's second and third lines and strong points in rear. Shortly before seven o'clock, the 60th Division had broken right through the enemy defences by the sea, and had reached, and established a bridgehead at the Wadi Nahr el Falyk, a mile or so behind the enemy line. Engineers and pioneers got to work at once, and in a very short space of time had made roads and bridges through the enemy trench system, and over the Nahr el Falyk, by which cavalry and guns could be pushed forward. At 7.30 the cavalry passed through on their dash for the tactical points behind the enemy's lines.

Meanwhile, all along the line our infantry had taken their first objectives with little opposition, the enemy having been taken completely by surprise. The whole line advanced to a maximum depth of 5 miles, and then swung to the right pivoting on Rafat. Such opposition as was encountered was met with at the strong points well behind the front line, where the enemy had had the time and opportunity to man his defences. For example, both at El Tireh and at Kalkilieh, stub-

orn resistance was encountered. Thus the line swung right-
anded into the hills, crumpling up the whole enemy line west
f Rafat. The 60th Division, after their break through,
narched for the greater part of the day, and, by 5.30 in the
fternoon, had reached Tul Keram. Our line, that evening,
an approximately south and north from Rafat to Tul Keram.

The cavalry passing through the gaps broken at the sea and
lose to Tabsor, pushed rapidly northward along the Coastal
Plain. Some of them made for Tul Keram, and, passing
hence up the Valley towards Nablus, had already reached
Anebta before dark, cutting off large bodies of the retreating
nemy with guns and transport between Tul Keram and the
ailway junction at Messudieh. Another strong cavalry
orce moved farther north. They passed through the moun-
ains east of Mount Carmel that night, by the Musmus Pass
Megiddo), and, early on the following morning, the 20th, they
harged the enemy holding the northern exit of the Pass and
lebouched on to the Plain of Esdraelon (Armageddon).

These seized the railway junction at El Afule. Some pushed
on eastwards towards the Jordan and captured Beisan (Beth-
han), some northwards and captured Nazareth, while some,
urning southwards, took Jenin in reverse. By nightfall on
he 20th all these tactical points were in our possession.

Yet another exploit remains to be chronicled. Far away
across the eastern desert, but beautifully co-ordinated, and
working as part of one great machine, moved a raiding force
of the Arab troops of Hussein, King of the Hejaz. At the
critical moment these swooped down upon the junction at
Deraa, where they destroyed the railway in all directions,
completely depriving the enemy of their main line of retirement.

Throughout the operations our airmen had the time of their
ives. Some hovered all day over the enemy aerodrome at
Jenin, and effectually prevented enemy machines from leaving
he ground. Some maintained contact between the infantry

and the higher command. Some, flying low, bombed and machine-gunned the retreating Turks, and completed their confusion.

The advance was continued on the 20th. On this day, the 10th Division, which had hitherto remained stationary to the right of Rafat, moved forward in a north-easterly direction, taking in rear the strong enemy position at Furkha. The whole line was now advancing and driving the retreating Turks towards Samaria and Nablus, and down the roads leading northwards and eastwards from these points. By the evening of the 20th, the Turkish resistance had collapsed everywhere on the west of the Jordan, except on the Turkish left in the Jordan Valley. Our right wing had advanced slightly, and occupied a line from near El Mugheir to Es Sawieh, while our left wing had swung round and reached the line Bidieh-Baka-Messudieh Junction—that is to say, we were gradually closing in on Nablus from the south, south-west, and west. Owing to the tactical positions behind the enemy lines having been seized by our cavalry, all avenues of escape which might have been open to the enemy had been closed, except the fords across the Jordan between Beisan and Jisr-ed-Damieh.

By the 21st, the retreating Turks had become a demoralized rabble, fleeing to the fords of the Jordan, like the discomfited Midianites, under Oreb and Zeeb, had fled more than three thousand years before from the pursuit of Gideon. Those who fled down the northward road were captured and collected by our cavalry at Jenin. Those who fled down the eastward road by the Wadi Fara, hoping to reach the still open ford at Jisr-ed-Damieh, met with a more cruel fate. This road led down a steep and narrow gorge, dominated by the heights east of Nablus. A brigade of the 10th Division was rushed forward by a forced march, and seized these heights, effectually closing the trap. Our airmen had already got the situation well in hand here, and the road soon became a veritable

hambles. The enemy had been forced or shepherded by our
ifantry into this bottle-neck, and our airmen, swooping down
o 200 feet and bombing the head of the column, soon made the
oad impassable. That accomplished, they flew up and down
he struggling column, bombing and machine-gunning without
t or hindrance. It seemed as though the unspeakable Turk
ad at last been delivered over to vengeance in this Valley of
eath. An eye-witness [1] describes the scene.

" In no section of Napoleon's retreat from Moscow could
here have been a more terrible picture of hopeless and irre-
ievable defeat. In this area alone, eighty-seven guns of vari-
us calibres, and fully a thousand horse and oxen-drawn vehicles,
early a hundred motor-lorries, cars, field-kitchens, water
arts, and a mass of other impedimenta blocked the road, with
he carcases of thousands of animals and the bodies of dead
urks and Germans."

On the 22nd, our cavalry moved up the Jordan Valley and
ized the ford at Jisr-ed-Damieh, thus cutting off the last
ossible means of escape. Prisoners were surrendering in
iousands. They looked weak and exhausted ; in many
ises they had fled over a parched country and beneath a
urning sun for three or four days, without touching a drop
f water. Their plight was pitiable. By that evening, the
urkish armies west of the Jordan had ceased to exist.

There still remained the Turkish 4th army in Eastern Pales-
ne. An expedition, consisting largely of cavalry, was sent
gainst them. These crossed the Jordan Valley, and, moving
p the eastern slopes, on the 23rd September captured Es
lt, and, on the 26th, Amman. A day or two later, the
urkish force south of Amman, about 10,000 strong, sur-
ndered. The remainder of the Turkish 4th army tried to
ithdraw. They were closely pursued by our cavalry and
rmen, and, to some extent, cut off by the Arab forces of the
ing of the Hejaz. Many prisoners were taken from this

---

[1] Mr. W. T. Massey, Official Correspondent with the E.E.F.

army, while, such as could do so, made their escape to Damascus.

The whole of Palestine, south of, and including the Plain of Esdraelon, was now in the hands of the British and their Arab allies. But there was still work to be done in a sweep forward towards Damascus. The Turks had some reserves at Damascus, and with these, and the remnants of their 4th army, they attempted to check our advance against that city. Accordingly, they sent a small force down to the Upper Jordan, that is, to the river north of the Sea of Galilee. This force, which consisted of Germans, Turks and Circassians, was rushed down from Damascus in motor-lorries, in order to deny the crossing at Jisr Benat Yakub. They blew up the bridge and covered the crossing with machine guns. On the 27th our cavalry, pushing north from Tiberias, swam the river both to the south and to the north of this crossing, and surprised and captured many of the enemy. They then, with armoured cars, pushed forward along the main Tiberias—Damascus road.

On the same day, other cavalry joined hands with the Arab army at Deraa. From this point, also, cavalry and armoured cars pushed northward. It seemed a question whether this force or that from Jisr Benat Yakub would be the first to reach Damascus, as both forces were rapidly approaching the city from the south and south-west respectively. The advance was still disputed by enemy rear guards, from whom prisoners and guns were captured. The enemy rear-guards were defeated, and, by the evening of the 30th, the city was partially surrounded.

Early on the morning of the 1st October, a British force and a portion of the Arab army of King Hussein occupied the city of Damascus.

In the course of a fortnight the enemy line had been broken Samaria, Galilee, Eastern Palestine and Damascus had been conquered; three Turkish armies had been destroyed, with a loss of their entire war material, and over 350 guns and 71,000 prisoners had been captured.

CHAPTER XVIII

CONCLUSION

SERIOUS fighting had practically finished with the capture of Damascus. The northward flight of the Turks continued, closely pursued by our cavalry and armoured cars. A Division of infantry was brought forward in support, but the difficulties of supplying a large force so far away from a base made it impossible to bring forward the infantry in any strength. Australians rounded up a Turkish column some miles north of Damascus, and a few thousand more prisoners were captured. Beyrout, the port of Damascus, was abandoned without a blow, and, on the 6th October, was occupied by the allies. A Division of French troops was landed here, and, thereafter, this port became the main channel of supply for the troops operating in Northern Syria.

Our forces pushed on northwards, meeting with little or no opposition, and occupying Baalbek, Tripolis and Homs. A Turkish force, under General Liman von Sanders, and estimated at about 12,000, concentrated a few miles south of Aleppo, where they threatened to offer some resistance. The advance northward was, however, unopposed. The enemy had constructed trenches covering Aleppo, and at first showed signs of holding them. But, after our armoured cars had got into touch, and our airmen had bombed them, the enemy decided to evacuate, and withdrew to the hills towards Alexandretta. Aleppo was entered by our cavalry on the 26th October, and the station was seized at Muslimie, the junction of the Baghdad Railway. By these captures we had made ourselves masters of the main line of communications with Constantinople of the Turkish armies in Mesopotamia.

Their armies virtually destroyed, the Turks now concluded an armistice, which took effect as from the 31st October. Their allies, the Bulgarians, who had suffered disastrous reverses in Macedonia, had just concluded an armistice; the Austrians were being badly beaten by the Italians and were clearly nearing the end; and the Germans were fast retiring from France and Belgium : so, with all hope of succour gone, the Turks had no alternative but to conclude an armistice, the terms of which practically amounted to unconditional surrender.

The terms of the armistice included the following. Immediate demobilization of the Turkish army, except troops required for the surveillance of the frontier and the maintenance of internal order ; the surrender of the garrisons of the Hejaz, Assir, Yemen, Syria and Mesopotamia, and the withdrawal of troops from Cilicia ; the surrender of all ports there ; occupation by the Allies of the Taurus Mountains tunnel system ; the allied control of all railways ; occupation by the Allies of any strategic points considered necessary for their security ; prohibition of destruction of military or similar material ; all Germans and Austrians to quit Turkey within a month ; Turkey to cease all relations with the Central Powers ; all allied prisoners in Turkish possession to be handed over unconditionally, but Turkish prisoners in the Allies' hands to be kept at the disposal of the Allies. In addition, all war vessels in Turkish waters were to be surrendered, the Dardanelles were to be opened, and free access secured for allied ships to all Turkish ports and exchanges and to the Black Sea.

A few days later, Austria threw in her hand, and, on the 11th November, an armistice was concluded with Germany. The Central Powers had surrendered. The greatest war in the history of the world had been brought to a close.

Will our campaign be passed down to history as " The

Last Crusade"? Presumably not. Throughout the campaign there was little or no religious animosity, except that the Moslem Turk extended no quarter to the Hindoo. To speak of this as a campaign of The Cross against The Crescent is untrue. The Turkish high command was controlled by Germans, so-called Christians. The British soldier fought with no less zest than when opposed to Turks. At the final battle, the Moslems, serving in our armies, by far outnumbered the Christians.

The close of the great war forms a fitting point at which to bring our story also to a close. Its aim has been a blend of history and reminiscence. Much has been set down here which would have been omitted from a history; much more has been omitted which a complete history would have contained. In particular I plead guilty to omitting names of units deserving of special mention. Generally their names have not been known to me; in such cases as they were known, I have feared that to mention them might have caused more jealousy than satisfaction. We each of us think, and rightly so, that our own unit does better than any other engaged. So, many a reader may be disappointed at finding no mention of the unit in which he is particularly interested. I can only refer him to the congratulatory telegrams which his unit received in the field, and which are doubtless preserved among the records of the regiment.

We have now completed our brief review of this campaign. We have seen its small beginnings in the defence of the Suez Canal, when Turkey, leaning upon Germany, a broken reed, vaunted herself in an attempt to conquer Egypt. We have traced the footsteps of the British army as, pushing back the invading Turk, it crept across the Desert. We have watched its struggles on the frontier of Asia, culminating in the victory of Gaza and Beersheba. We have followed its progress in the onward sweep, which conquered Jerusalem, and watched it through succeeding months of trial, patience and disappointment. Finally, we have seen it destroy the remnants of the Turkish armies, and, in one great rush, conquer the whole of Northern Syria. Proud, indeed, should those of us feel who have been privileged to play a part in this campaign.

INDEX

147

Printed in Great Britain for ROBERT SCOTT, *Publisher,* PATERNOSTER ROW, LONDON,
by BUTLER & TANNER, FROME

CPSIA information can be obtained at www.ICGtesting.com
Printed in the USA
BVOW08s2316210616

452931BV00001BA/43/P